Map Included

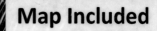

D1246033

INDIA SOUTH

CHINA

AFGHA-
NISTAN

PAKISTAN   NEPAL   BHUTAN
IRAN   New
            Delhi
                                BANGLA-
Tropic of Cancer   DESH
                       Kolkata
OMAN   MYAN-
        Mumbai   **INDIA**   MAR
Arabian
Sea   **INDIA**   Chennai
           South

                       SRI LANKA
INDIAN OCEAN

WITHDRAWN

www.marco-polo.com

THE
TOURING APP

shows you the way...
including routes and offline maps!

FREE!

GET MORE OUT OF YOUR MARCO POLO GUIDE

IT'S AS SIMPLE AS THIS

1 go.marco-polo.com/inds

2 download and discover

GO!

WORKS OFFLINE!

SYMBOLS

 Insider Tip

★ Highlight

●●●● Best of ...

☼ Scenic view

◍ Responsible travel: for
ecological or fair trade
aspects

(*) Telephone numbers
that are not toll-free

**PRICE CATEGORIES
HOTELS**

Expensive	over 6100 Rs
Moderate	3050–6100 Rs
Budget	under 3050 Rs

The prices are for two people
sharing per night, including
breakfast

**PRICE CATEGORIES
RESTAURANTS**

Expensive	over 915 Rs
Moderate	535–915 Rs
Budget	535 Rs

The prices are for a main
meal without drinks

CONTENTS

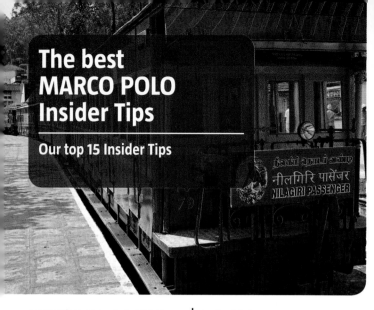

The best MARCO POLO Insider Tips

Our top 15 Insider Tips

INSIDER TIP Saturday night in Goa

While others sleep, in Goa you can go shopping. Enjoy a very special atmosphere, partying, bartering and marvelling at the *Arpora Saturday Night Bazaar* → **p. 36**

INSIDER TIP City of the future

Spiritual freedom thanks to yoga and meditation at the Sri Aurobindo spiritual community *Auroville*. Around 2400 people from 40 countries live in this 'universal city' → **p. 105, 116**

INSIDER TIP Karaoke under the stars

In *Joet's Guest House* on Bogmalo Bay, every Friday evening DJ Emmanuel plays music – it's karaoke time! Goans are fantastic singers, and the atmosphere is also fantastic → **p. 41**

INSIDER TIP Hot & spicy

Nutmeg, cardamom, vanilla, cinnamon and sandalwood – exotic fragrances at the *spice market* in Kochi → **p. 71**

INSIDER TIP From villains to conservationists

Go *trekking* with former ivory smugglers and poachers in Thekkady: no one is more familiar with the tracks of the elephants, or can better spot the signs of a tiger → **p. 128**

INSIDER TIP Thousands of coconuts for Ganesh

Every morning, generous offerings are taken to the elephant-headed Hindu god at the *Pazhavangadi Ganapathy Temple* → **p. 86**

INSIDER TIP River islands by bicycle

Far from car exhaust fumes and the hubbub of city traffic, you can enjoy a bicycle tour and explore the idyllic islands of *Divar* and *Chorao* in the Mandovi River, close to Goa's capital Panaji – a wonderfully relaxing trip → **p. 123**

INSIDER TIP Frolicking around

In the evening, dolphins come out to play in the sea off the secluded *Agonda beach* → **p. 38**

BEST OF ...

FOR FREE

● *An early start to the day with yoga*
From 6am–8am, at 26 different public spaces in Chennai, e.g. Panagal Park and Marina Beach, you can take part in *free yoga classes*. The idea came from the former mayor, who had the good health of the citizenry at heart → **p. 129**

● *Massage included*
In the spice gardens of Goa, tours also include free, relaxing *massages*. Of course, there is the ulterior motive that you'll later purchase the requisite oils, but you don't have to → **p. 43**

● *Silent Noise Parties*
Dancing at night, barefoot on the sand, with headphones on – that's both romantic and considerate. And it's easy on the wallet: the *open air discos in Palolem* in Goa offer free entry → **p. 39**

● *First the rice harvest, then the entertainment*
Once the rice has been gathered in, the farmers around Hampi organise *ox-cart races* and *bullfights*. The animals don't suffer because they are not pierced by a spear. The Torero's prize being the money and sweets that he manages to pluck from the head of the bull. And you can also take part and enjoy South Indian traditions up close → **p. 53**

● *End the day with fresh shrimps*
Buy some freshly caught shrimps straight from the Chinese fishing nets (photo) in Kochi and have them prepared at the stall. They'll cost you a pound at most and you'll sit on the sand with the bag in your hand and watch as the giant nets are silhouetted against the sunset – just stunning! → **p. 70**

● *More than 300 concerts for free*
At the *Chennai Music and Dance Festival*, classical music and traditional dances are performed at more than 100 venues, with at least 300 concerts. And it doesn't cost a thing, though small donations are, of course, always welcome → **p. 133**

●●●● Dots in guidebook refer to 'Best of ...' tips

ONLY IN SOUTH INDIA
Unique experiences

● *When Indian men go dancing*
Kathakali, the best-known dance drama in South India, is noted for the colourful make-up and elaborate costumes of the male-only performers (photo). You are welcome to watch the painstaking make-up process, and of course the dances themselves, which recreate scenes from ancient Hindu epics → **p. 73**

● *Temporary tattoo*
In the model village of *Dakshinachitra* near Chennai, you can see demonstrations of typical Indian handicrafts. While you're there, you can also have elaborate henna mehndi patterns painted on your hands → **p. 102**

● *Spiritual shopping*
Pondicherry is a real shopper's paradise when it comes to basic spiritual requirements. This is mainly due to the *Sri Aurobindo shops,* which sell clothes, bags, jewellery, incense sticks, oils and high quality handmade paper, all made in the nearby ashram at Auroville → **p. 105**

● *Receive a blessing*
In the temples visitors can request a mark, which is painted on the forehead with ashes, and a bracelet tied around the wrist that must be worn until it falls off. At *Pazhavangadi Ganapathy Temple* in Trivandrum, you can receive both → **p. 86**

● *Riding pillion through Goa*
When in Goa you can hire a motorbike rider who will take you everywhere on the back of his bike or Vespa. It's inexpensive, fun and an unusual way to get around. You can find *two-wheeler taxi stands* everywhere → **p. 41**

● *Farewell on the beach*
These *ceremonies* may make you feel uneasy, but will show you a real piece of India. You have to get up early though to watch the priests at work on *Varkala beach* in Kerala. Families arrive with the ashes of their recently departed, so they can be blessed and then scattered in the sea → **p. 88**

ONLY IN

BEST OF ...

● *Walking in the rain*
At the *Monsoon Splash*, the hill tribes of northeast Kerala celebrate the monsoon rains with particular abandon. And you can join in too, with walks in the rain, mud football or crab races → **p. 84**

● *Shopping South Indian style*
You can get lost in the covered bazaar near the *Sri Meenakshi Sundareshwarar Temple* in Madurai. Time flies as you wander among all the fragrances, colours and gorgeous materials → **p. 106**

● *Doubly effective*
Because the warm dampness opens up the pores in the skin to absorb creams and oils, Ayurveda practitioners believe that the *Monsoon season* is the best time of year for a cure. There is the additional consideration that patients can concentrate fully on their treatments, rather than swim or sunbathe (photo) → **p. 64**

● *More than Bollywood*
Indian movies are not just Bollywood. And every small town has its own cinema, where the audience enthusiastically participates, laughing, crying and clapping. Go along and experience it all at first hand – in Chennai, Ooty and many other places → **p. 101, 112**

● *Market for all the senses*
Around the halls of the *Devaraja Fruit & Vegetable Market* in Mysore you'll experience the real India. Sample the juicy (peeled!) tropical fruits, take photographs of the colourful spice cones, close your eyes and absorb the intense floral scents → **p. 62**

● *The power of water*
The *Jog Falls* in Karnataka are at their most impressive during the monsoon season. Then the six separate cascades merge into one, as enormous quantities of water drop thunderously to depths of 250 m/820 ft → **p. 56**

RAIN

RELAX AND CHILL OUT
Take it easy and spoil yourself

● *Relax with a good conscience*
The legendary Om Beach is the location of the *Swaswara Yoga and Ayurveda Resort*. In this charming hotel they don't just focus on your wellbeing, but thanks to strict environmental guidelines also take care of the surroundings – a totally holistic experience → **p. 59**

● *Dine in peaceful harmony*
At the thatched *Blue Ginger Restaurant* in Bangalore those travelling alone have two goldfish delivered to the table in a bowl. Such dining partners aid relaxation: you don't have to make conversation and you can still have pleasant company → **p. 48**

● *Paradise from a boat*
The *Pichavaram Forest* near Chidambaram is the world's second-largest mangrove forest and a unique place for ecotourism. The boat takes you right away from civilisation and through a luxuriant wilderness → **p. 104**

● *Vantage point*
The best place to chill for the evening is in an *open air café on the Varkala cliffs* (photo) in Kerala. Sit with your feet up in the first row, as you watch the sun dipping into the sea. And enjoy the spectacular panoramic view out to sea and over the sand, which soon becomes a stage for entranced dancers → **p. 89**

● *In good hands*
A visit to the *Millennium Beauty Parlour* in Margao is an all-round, feel-good experience. You can spend an entire day here, with natural hair packs and wonderful massages and peelings → **p. 39**

● *Chilling out on a houseboat*
In the gloriously enchanting *Backwaters of Kerala*, the best and most relaxing way to enjoy the tropical environment with its rich flora and fauna is from the deck of a houseboat. During the journey, they will spoil you with delicious regional specialities, freshly prepared on board → **p. 92**

11

INTRODUCTION

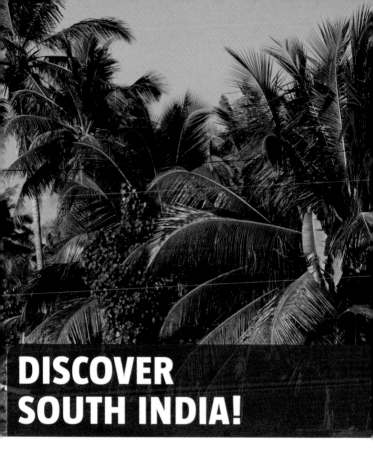

DISCOVER SOUTH INDIA!

South India gets under your skin. It's a place where the air is soft and velvety, full of promise. Those who really engage with it will also learn much about themselves. A journey through this *magical, sensory land* is like visiting your inner self. Witness a temple ceremony and you are likely to lose all sense of time and space. Watching the fishermen putting out to the Arabian Sea in their *ancient catamarans*, you will feel as if you are in a time warp. Ayurvedic oil massages can help to induce a state of weightlessness, and everywhere you go, bustle and stress are replaced by a much calmer rhythm. And then there are the *smiles*, which are so infectious that in the end you just can't resist.

Whether landing in Chennai (Madras), in Panaji, in Bengaluru (Bangalore) or in Thiruvananthapuram (Trivandrum), new arrivals will be almost bowled over by a surge of *exotic images*. Heavy is the *smell of coconut* in the palm groves of Kerala, mixed with the opium-sweet fragrance of the white almond blossom. *Traffic congestion* in the cities, accompanied by a continuous blaring of horns, takes some getting used to. Apparent contradictions are a matter of course for locals. The phone shops are gradually disappearing. But instead you will find *internet cafés* on every corner

Photo: The Backwaters of Kerala

and almost every hotel offers WiFi free of charge. And women wearing **traditional saris but talking into a mobile phone** is a common sight on the streets. Rolling into Mysore aboard the **Golden Chariot** luxury train, you will have a close encounter with the poorest of the poor sleeping on the station platform. But only tourists bother to take any notice of them. In contrast, the number of willing hands who seem to know exactly what guests want, is extravagant by European standards. South India is at first tiring, because it **assaults the senses** in such an unfamiliar way. Relaxation will only begin when you start to let go and open your mind to the region's intoxicating mix – the memory will stay with you forever.

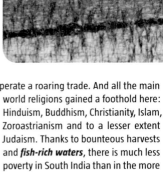

Over the course of the centuries, **conquerors from Europe** were keen to grab a slice of India for themselves: the Dutch, the Portuguese the English and the French ... No wonder, this was fertile ground that yielded enough **fruit and spices, as well as precious minerals**, to operate a roaring trade. And all the main world religions gained a foothold here: Hinduism, Buddhism, Christianity, Islam, Zoroastrianism and to a lesser extent Judaism. Thanks to bounteous harvests and **fish-rich waters**, there is much less poverty in South India than in the more barren north. The level of education is higher, and in Kerala illiteracy hardly exists. Especially exciting is the **mix of cultures**. While young whizz-kids are busy developing their software in Bangalore, around

The Europeans grabbed territory for themselves

268–233 BC
King Ashoka rules over the entire Indian empire

AD 550–1190
Start of the Indian Middle Ages, with the rise of South India

1498
Navigator and explorer Vasco da Gama lands at Calicut in present-day Kerala, thereby ushering in the colonial period

1746
The French conquer Madras

From 1756
From its bases in Calcutta, Madras and Bombay, the British East India Company subjugates large parts of India

The fertile soil yields a plentiful harvest – rice is still the No. 1 food

250 km/155 mi away in the Nilgiri Mountains the *Toda tribe* still clings to its ancient traditions that have been handed down for thousands of years. Like a magnet for people all over the world, sadhus, gurus and yogis attract *those in search of life's meaning*. In many ashrams, pilgrims follow the teachings and vision of their master. Auroville near Pondicherry was founded in 1968 by Mother Mira Alfassa, the wife of the philosopher Sri Aurobindo. Today, her *model spiritual commune* accommodates around 2400 people from more than 40 countries.

At one time, visitors to South India were either student travellers or here for a beach holiday. Nowadays, people tend to have broader interests and hardly anyone stay-

1858
Control of India passes from the East India Company to the British Crown, whose representative is the Viceroy

1877
The British Queen Victoria becomes Empress of India

1885
Founding of the National Congress

1920
Mahatma Gandhi calls for the non-violent overthrow of British rule

1947
India gains independence. Jawaharlal Nehru is the first prime minister

ing at the beaches of Goa or Kerala will come away without at least having taken a stroll through the **historic Old Goa** or seeing the magnificent **Padmanabha Swamy Temple** in Kerala's capital, Trivandrum. Anyone interested in the living history and architecture of holy sites will be impressed by the **sea temples of Mamallapuram**, by the stunning temple complex of Hampi, the fairytale palace of the Maharajas in Mysore and the magnificent Meenakshi temple in Madurai.

Many hotels, even small ones, are more than just somewhere to spend the night. Often there will be an Indian version of a **spa zone** with at least one massage table or a few magic tinctures to revive tired feet and weary spirits. More effective over the long term are Ayurveda treatments involving special diets, which can work wonders — provided you stick rigidly to the regime.

All the great world religions gained a foothold

Increasing numbers of outdoor enthusiasts and eco-tourists head for the larger national parks to 'shoot' **elephants and leopards** on their photo safaris: in game reserves like Periyar in Kerala; Molem and Bhagvan Mahavir, which straddles the border between Goa, Karnataka, Kerala and Tamil Nadu in the Western Ghats; in Bandipur, Nagarhole and Kabini in Karnataka. Trekking tours take in the **enchanted world of the jungle** and rainforest. Kerala's Backwaters, the dense network of almost 2000 km/1240 mi of waterways, lakes and lagoons, create another unique attraction. Over a **thousand houseboats** in Alappuzha wait on tourists to take them along what were once important commercial transport arteries.

And all visitors succumb to the **temptation that is shopping**. Almost every holidaymaker flies home with double the amount of luggage. Tea straight from the factory, spices from colourful markets, decorative **statues of gods** made out of bronze or sandalwood, silk blouses, cotton fabrics with exotic designs, pashmina shawls, real gold and silver jewellery, and sparkling false gold. The **cotton and silk fabrics** from Chennai (Madras) and nearby Kanchipuram are among the most beautiful and finest materials to be found in all India. Chennai is also the centre of the **leather industry**. Because most products are exported to the west, you can also find all the latest fashion in the shops, at prices well below what you'd pay in London. As a shopper's paradise, India simply can't be beaten!

1950 Indian Constitution adopted

1956 The former princely states of Cochin, Malabar and Travancore join to become the state of Kerala

1961 End of Portuguese colonial rule in Goa

1973 Merging of Coorg and the states of Bombay, Madras and Hyderabad into present-day Karnataka

2004 The Sikh Dr. Manmohan Singh is voted India's first non-Hindu prime minister

Whatever your particular priorities might be, Goa and Karnataka, Kerala and Tamil Nadu have more than enough variety, and all year round as well. High season in Goa is considered to be October, the *start of the dry season*, which goes on to May/June. But if you've ever seen the film 'Monsoon Wedding', you'll know how romantic

It looks artistic but it's hard work: fishermen mend the nets

a *warm tropical downpour* can be. Many beach hotels offer special *monsoon deals*. Anyway, it hardly ever pours down the entire day, heavy showers alternate with sunny spells, and certainly anyone who is interested in experiencing India without all the foreign tourists, wants to get to know the locals better and would like to sample the *slightly melancholic mood*, should come during the monsoon. But that's India for intermediates or advanced.

2010
Rampant corruption is the dominant domestic issue

2011
1.21 billion people live in the world's biggest democracy, 181 million more than at the census in 2001

2014
Narendra Modi becomes the 15th Prime Minister, his BJP wins the parliamentary election with an absolute majority. He is regarded as a bearer of hope – especially for India's closer relationship with Pakistan. He is, however, a staunch conservative Hindu nationalist

WHAT'S HOT

1 Endless clubbing

Let's rave! Goa parties are celebrated around the world but they're still best at the original source. The website *WUG (www.whatsupgoa.com)* lists the most popular parties, best live bands and addresses. Like the hip *Hill Top*, outdoor club in Vagator. Themed parties are celebrated on five floors in the grand *Nyex Beach Club* at Anjuna beach. The beach hut *Curlies* is the place to go for trance parties at South Anjuna Beach. Youngsters hang out in *Cohiba Bar* in Candolim and in *Boomerang Bar* in Colva.

Cool grapes

2

Viniculture Since India rediscovered winemaking in the 1990s, production and consumption have heavily increased. Young, creative winemakers start up with exciting experiments and invite you to tastings. Young city-dwellers and business people find it cool to order a fine drop of local wine with dinner. Wine-growing areas are in Nashik/Maharashtra, Karnataka, Goa and the foothills of the Himalaya. Indian Sauvignon Blanc, Chenin Blanc, Shiraz and Cabernet Sauvignon are now even exported.

3 Art from the can

Graffiti It was once a sub-culture, but in India graffiti has also become an art form: street art is hip! Indian and international sprayers leave behind their tags everywhere. Dismal Indian inner-cities are becoming more vibrant thanks to the *murals*. Even if it's not legal: in India, sprayers find willing home owners who proudly showcase the result. Brightly coloured wall painting, especially with gaudy advertising, has a long tradition in India. Find out where South India's graffiti is on display at *graffitiinindia.com*.

There are lots of new things to discover in South India. A few of the most interesting are listed below

Urban farmers

Green fingers It isn't just Bengaluru's Botanic Gardens that are worth a visit. On request, some private residents will let you have a look at their roof gardens; urban gardening is now very fashionable in India's big cities. Bloggers and websites such as 🔍 *www.cityfarmer.info/category/india* deal with topics involving choice of seed and fertiliser, but there are also courses and even school lessons on the subject *(photo)*. The author Dr. B. N. Viswanath and his 🔍 *Garden City Farmers (enquiries tel. 94486 2 95 28 | www.gardencityfarmers.org)* in Bengaluru organise one-day workshops. It's about creating a sustainable future and making a stand against environmental pollution. In Chennai you can also join plant-themed walks *(madraswanderer.com)*.

Stylish jewellery

East meets West Indian women are known for their beautiful jewellery, pieces in which every stone and every shape has a meaning. Contemporary jewellery designers are inspired by tradition and produce dangly earrings, necklaces and bracelets that make heads turn on the streets of New York and London. But the items still have the typical oriental look. Good places to go for beautifully made jewellery include *Gehna (Harrington Rd, Chetpet | Chennai)* and *Amrapali (amrapalijewels.com)*, with outlets in Chennai and Bengaluru. Or the traditional jeweller *Ganjam (Bldg. No. 63, Palace Rd, Vasanth Nagar | Bengaluru)* as well as two outlets of *Anmol* in Bengaluru *(www.anmoljewellers.in) (Photo)*.

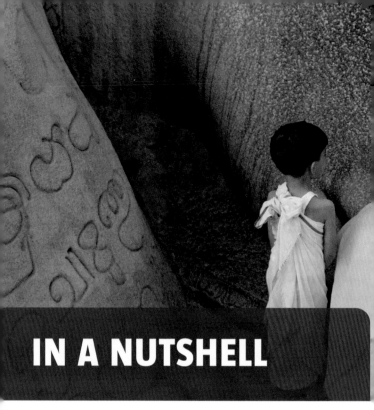

IN A NUTSHELL

BEAUTY

Visiting an Indian beauty parlour is a wonderful experience and, even if hygiene standards away from the good hotels leave something to be desired, the traditional applications are unmatched. You could easily spend a whole day there, having a facial with purely herbal ingredients, an epilation using the ancient threading method, and enjoying a relaxing head, body or foot massage. Henna is not just used as a dye but also as a healthy hair pack, enriched with yoghurt, egg, lemon and scented oils. The treatments cost a fraction of what you would pay in western Europe. So even in the less salubrious establishments, you'll probably be quite happy to close your eyes.

CASTE SYSTEM

The caste system was first mentioned in sacred texts *(veda)* as long ago as 1200 BC. Officially, since the adoption of the modern constitution in 1950, it has been abolished, but it still exists in the minds of many Indians. For example, they find it unthinkable to have a marriage between people of a different caste. Even today, a person's social background can be determined from their family name, which provides information on former status. The caste system consists of four main castes *(varnas)*, which are further divided into many sub-groups or *jatis*. Brahmins, traditionally the spiritual and intellectual elite, the priests and interpreters of holy scripts, occupy the highest-ranking

**Between poverty and riches:
stark contrasts characterise the south of the
world's most populous democracy**

varna. The second-highest caste is that of the *kshatryas,* made up of warriors, princes and high officials. Traders and farmers were the *vaishas*, while the *shudras* included labourers, tenant farmers and slaves.

Forming a special caste of their own were the so-called *parias* or *dalits* – the Untouchables. They were, for example, denied access to the temple and couldn't even cast their shadow on the food of someone belonging to a higher caste.

ECONOMY

India's economy is booming. With a growth rate of 7.4 % in the financial year 2014/2015, India is one of the world's fastest growing economies. In terms of GDP, by the middle of this century it is expected to lie in third place after China and the USA. India already plays a major role in the global market, deriving much of its strength from the IT industry.

And yet it is still the case that despite the emergence of a burgeoning middle class in India, there is nowhere else with such a large gap between rich and poor. The subcontinent might have the world's largest number of millionaires and billionaires, but the average annual per capita income is just 560 £/725 US$. An astonishing 28 percent of the population lives below the poverty line of 0.77 £/1 US$ per day, preserving India's status as a developing country.

Indian women between tradition and contemporary fashion

ENVIRONMENT

Several resort hotels, not just the 🌐 *cgh earth group* that has been at the forefront of developments in ecotourism and sustainability, but smaller resorts as well, have developed a high degree of environmental awareness. It will look spotless too at other accommodation, including the stretches of beach that belong to them. But as soon as you leave the clean zone, it's over with the environmental awareness. Plastic bottles and bags litter the ground, and no one feels the need to get rid of them. Survival is more important than refuse disposal, they say. But there is hope. Jose Dominic, founding member of the 🌐 *Ecotourism Society of India,* works in the field of public awareness. His society organises presentations all over the country, because it's clear that rubbish isn't just a problem for local people but it also represents a threat to the tourist industry. According to its director, the emphasis of the ecotourism initiative is on sustainability. Its aim is to involve the inhabitants of the different areas, so that they too benefit from tourism. It is also looking at ways in which waste could be converted into electricity. There are also problems in the Backwaters of Kerala, where villagers do their washing with lots of detergent and also throw their rubbish in the channels. 'We want to increase awareness of the need for a clean environment there as well, for houseboats there's already a law against the disposing of waste in the water,' says Dominic.

FASHION

The Asia look is in. Glittering *bangles* for your wrist, bags with pictures of Indian gods, colourful, beaded slippers and embroidered tunics, are all must-haves for fashion conscious ladies. At parties in Goa, guests even wear costumes that look like they're straight out of Bollywood movies. Indian fashion designers have long since joined the ranks of European labels. Sabyasachi Mukherjee, who designs under the *Sabyasachi* label, shows off his creations during New York

Fashion Week and is promoted by Sotheby's as a top fashion designer. But cheap hippie-style clothes are also very popular. In the resorts of Kovalam and Varkala, at the Anjuna fleamarket and at Ingo's Night Market between Baga and Anjuna in Goa, multi-coloured cotton and silk skirts flap in the breeze, as do wide, often wrapped-round trousers that are incredibly convenient for travelling. Then there are cashmere sweaters from Nepal and colourful cardigans from Tibet.

Another tip for female tourists who would like to wear a sari during their trip to India is to make sure an Indian woman shows you how to 'wrap' it correctly; otherwise, the folds won't fall in the right places and the triangle at the back will be too low. And that would look ridiculous! More practical and every bit as exotic is the *salwar kameez*, a pair of narrow trousers with a matching knee-length tunic.

FILM INDUSTRY

Bollywood in Mumbai (Bombay) is well-known; the fact that there is also a Kollywood, less so. It is based in Chennai (Madras) in Tamil Nadu and ever since 1916 it has been producing films that are mainly in the Tamil language, with the first Tamil talkie coming out in 1931. The name is derived from the Hindi film industry from Mumbai and the district in Chennai – Kodanbakkan – where the studios are located. Kollywood films, however, tend to focus on action and martial arts rather than on Bollywood-style love scenes, which is partly why they are so big in Japan. The most successful actors of Tamil films also included the later Chief Minister of Tamil Nadu, Marudur Gopalamenon Ramachandran. Another Chief Minister, Dr Kalaignar Karunanidhi, wrote screenplays and starred in roles alongside Ramachandran.

LANGUAGES

Because each state has its own language with many different dialects, some even with different written forms, Hindi was designated as India's official language. Due to colonial history, the second official language is English, which is spoken mainly by the elite but also by increasing numbers of the burgeoning middle class who need to communicate internationally. As far as the main local languages of South India are concerned, *Konkani* is spoken in Goa, *Kannada* in Karnataka, the very quick-fire *Malayalam* in Kerala and *Tamil* in Tamil Nadu.

MUSIC

Forming the basis of classical Indian music is the *raga,* a basic melodic structure. The Sanskrit word translates as feeling or mood. So through its particular melody and range of tonal nuances, each raga conjures up a different mood. Similar to jazz, the musician has a lot of scope for improvisation. The versatile *sitar* often serves as the main instrument, while the rhythm is determined by the two-drum *tabla*. While classical music is often difficult for Western ears to grasp, the songs and dance music from Bollywood movies are currently very popular. Indian pop music is substantially influenced by the musical genre known as *bhangra*, which originates from the Punjab. You can hear bhangra in many Bollywood soundtracks. For example, the song *Mundian To Bach Ke* ('Beware of the Boys') by *Panjabi MC* took the European charts by storm. It even occupied the top spot in Italy. Mixed with house and reggae, bhangra is now an established part of the club scene in South Asia.

NATURAL DISASTERS

The tsunami unleashed by the Indian Ocean earthquake on 26 December 2004 caused massive damage in South India. Thousands of people died along the coast, while thousands more, notably fishermen, lost their livelihoods. Of the official Indian death toll of over 16,000 registered victims, some 7800 alone were from the state of Tamil Nadu. Today, virtually all traces have been removed, although many of the affected fishermen still haven't received any compensation. This is also an earthquake region, although in the South the tremors are usually weaker than in the North or in Central India. Flooding often happens during the monsoon season, like in 2015. The heaviest downpours are in Western Ghats. On the other hand, in particularly hot summers there are long periods of drought, so even the hotels are required to save water.

POPULATION AND POLITICS

At the last census, 1.21 billion people were recorded as living in India. The population had risen by 181 million from the time of the previous census in 2001. That makes India the world's most populous parliamentary democracy. The enormous country is made up of 29 states and seven union territories including in the south Puducherry, the Andaman and Nicobar Islands and Lakshadweep. Its capital is New Delhi. In contrast to the federal states, each with its own local government, the union territories are subject to direct control fom the government in New Delhi. In order to erase the last vestiges of colonialism, since the mid-1990s many cities have been renamed in their respective local languages. Some names such as Chennai – the former Madras – bear no resemblance to their old name; others, such as Udhagamandalam for Ooty and Thiruvananthapuram for Trivandrum, are so cumbersome, that even the inhabitants continue to use the old names. At the end of May 2014, after ten years, the ruling party UPA was replaced by the Bharatiya Janata (BJP – the Indian People's Party). Their leading candidate Narendra Modi became India's 15th Prime Minister – previously, a humble tea seller. The President is the lawyer and former Finance Minister Pranab Mukherjee.

SPIRITUALITY

In India, faith and superstition merge together. Every practising Hindu goes to the temple to pray at least twice a day. And even enlightened businessmen will consult the 'house astrologer' before closing a deal to check that the timing is auspicious. Spirituality in India has a tradition stretching back more than 3000 years. Even today, through the doctrine of karma, it provides the poorest of the poor with the hope of better fortune in the next life. An ashram (literally: place of religious retreat) is a centre of contemplation, visited by disciples of a particular master, or guru. Depending on his individual philosophy he will lead his followers on a journey of spiritual and religious discovery, often aided by meditation and yoga. Sri Sathya Sai Baba (1926–2011) was revered even more strongly than a guru, namely as an *Avatar* – an incarnation of God. His ashrams in Puttaparthi/Andra Pradesh and in Whitefield/Karnataka still enjoy great popularity. His credo was: all religions are equally important. Known simply as 'Amma', Sri Mata Amritanandamayi was born in 1953 in Kerala and her ashram is located in the fishing village of Amrita. Always compassionate and caring towards everyone, she blesses those in search of healing and truth with a hug – worldwide she has now hugged more than 24 million people. Mother Meera was born in 1960 in Andra Pradesh, but now lives in Germany and on her travels there and abroad she blesses her followers with a touch on the temple.

WOMEN

It is quite a balancing act for Indian women to move between modernity and tradition. In the cities of South India, most young women now have a job or profession. Thanks to their financial independence, they also have much more self-confidence than just a few decades ago. However, some men still cannot cope with this transformation and persistently regard women and girls as defenceless sexual objects. Rape cases committed by individuals or gangs of men have recently been a sad indictment of this retro-minded attitude. In rural areas, girls have far fewer educational opportunities. While the constitution guarantees them equal rights with men, this is hardly apparent in everyday life. Here, the woman is still largely subordinate. Except in Goa, where young women can freely choose whom they want to marry, it is mainly still the parents who select a suitable match for their daughter in an arranged marriage. In the world of politics, by contrast, the transformation started in the days of Indira Gandhi, who was prime minister of India from 1966 to 1977 and again from 1980 to 1984. Since then, further important political posts have been filled by women. Between 2007 and 2012, for example, Prathiba Devisingh Patil was, as president, India's head of state.

In Thanjavur spiritual life is writ large: overall 90 temples welcome worshippers

FOOD & DRINK

Generally speaking, South Indian cuisine is much hotter than northern Indian. Coconut is a ubiquitous ingredient: it is present in many sauces, used for its oil and even appears in the form of alcohol, like *toddy* (palm wine) and *arrack*.

The signature dish is *thali,* which consists of a mound of rice, with up to 36 different vegetarian delights piled up in appetizing little heaps and traditionally *served on a banana leaf*. In Kerala this lavish dish is called *sadya*. It tastes best when you *eat with your fingers* (only with the right 'clean' hand), as is the norm in India. Hotel restaurants now serve up streamlined versions on a plate. However, when eaten from a banana leaf the taste is incomparably better, and of course more authentic.

Freshly caught *king prawns* and *lobster* from the sea are prepared in a variety of ways. Rice is the most important *staple* in South India. It is not only used as a grain but also as flour. Popular dishes include biryani*, mixed rice dishes with vegetables* and usually also meat. *Curries (karis)* originate from Tamil cuisine. The special taste is achieved by the use of *specific mixtures of spices*. These include curry leaves, tamarind, coriander, ginger, garlic, chillies, cinnamon, cloves, cardamom, cumin, fennel, aniseed, fenugreek seeds, nutmeg, coconut, turmeric and rose water. It has nothing much in common with the curry powder used in Europe.

The finest cuisine is in the *Chettinad region*. The best breakfast in India can

A treat for the taste buds: in the south of India every dish, every bite reveals another sensory experience

be enjoyed in Kerala. One speciality available all across India is the *dosa*, very thinly rolled **rice flour pancakes**, which is served with coconut chutney and spicy sambar sauce. While Kerala is renowned for having India's best **seafood**, Goan menus offer a variety of chicken dishes, unusual puddings and of course seafood specialities such as **prawn curry**. The native Goans learned how to prepare spicy sausage from the Portuguese. *Vindaloo* is derived from the Portuguese 'carne em vinha d'alhos', **meat marinated in wine and garlic**. The addition of red chillies and spices make the dish especially hot. In the sophisticated cuisine of Chettinad in Tamil Nadu, in addition to **typical Tamil** flavours there are influences from Burma, Indonesia and Europe. Be that as it may, young chefs are putting increasing emphasis on light cuisine. **Desserts** are often sugar- and fat-free, and made from cereals, fruit and lentils.

India is a fun place to travel for vegetarians. Because millions of Indians live

LOCAL SPECIALITIES

appam – simple rice pancakes

bhaji – vegetables fried in a batter of gram flour

chicken cafrial – diced chicken coated with a spicy sauce, a Goan speciality

chourisso – red-coloured sausages in Goa

chutney (chatni) – spicy to hot paste made of pickled fruit or vegetables and served with *thalis*

dhal – pulses, mostly red lentils

feni – schnapps made from cashews

garam masala – take care: a very hot mixture of spices!

idiyappam – also known as "string hoppers" made from rice flour pressed into noodle form and served for breakfast with spicy vegetable sauce

idli sambar – flat rice cake with a spicy sauce

jaggery – these brown lumps made from sugar cane are much healthier than sugar, contain many minerals, proteins and vitamins and are also used in Ayurvedic cuisine

kerala parippu – really a runny curry made of dhal, desiccated coconut, green and red chillies as well as ghee (clarified butter)

kurlleachi karti – crabmeat curry with dessicated coconut

masala – spice mixture for vegetables, *dosas*, salads and rice

murg masala – chicken with spices, nuts and yoghurt

pakora – vegetables or egg fried in batter

panir – unsalted white cheese cut into cubes

pappadam – thin cracker made from rice or lentil flour and fried in oil until crisp

pilau – spiced rice with vegetables

puttu – solid mound of rice flour and coconut, usually served for breakfast

rasam – spicy hot soup, usually made from tomatoes

roti – flat bread made from wheat, oats, millet or corn flour, excellent for soaking up sauces (photo right)

sambar – slightly runny side dish made from vegetables, lentils, chillies and tamarind

samosa – deep-fried pastry parcel usually filled with potato and peas but also with meat (photo left)

tandoori – chicken or other meat prepared in a cylindrical clay oven

thali – different dishes presented in small bowls – or on a banana leaf in Kerala

uppama – braised vegetables

without meat, the **vegetarian cuisine** is among the most varied and diverse in the world. For practising Hindus purity of mind and spirit also means **abstinence from meat**, fish, poultry, and often eggs as well. In every city, in every village there are several vegetarian restaurants. And every 'normal' *(non-veg)* restaurant either has a separate menu, if not a **separate seating area or dining room** for vegetarians. Those who can't tolerate hot and spicy food should ask for 'non spicy'. Incidentally, the restaurants are usually open daily from 12 noon until midnight.

The safest beverage is the refreshing juice of the **king coconut** – the young coconut. If you really want to be sure, you can bring along your own straw for drinking at the street stalls. Drinking soda with lemon juice and salt is a good way to combat salt loss. The same goes for **lassi** – whipped yogurt, often served with fruit, like mango *lassi* for example. **Beers such as Kingfisher** and *Golden Eagle* are brewed in India; they generally have a lower alcohol content than European beers. The Portuguese introduced wine to Goa as long ago as the 16th century, but in recent years India has made a name for itself **cultivating its own vines**. Experts speak of India's 'vine-growing triangle', which covers the regions of Nashik, Pune and Mumbai in Maharashtra. As far as quantity is concerned, this still doesn't match internationally-renowned wine-producing areas, but the quality can easily compete, with Indian Merlot, Sauvignon and Chardonnay receiving high praise at wine fairs. Thanks to state funding Indian wine production will experience continued growth. Even now, many wineries organise **tastings**. Tea is served at every opportunity. Because it is brewed strongly, it is drunk with milk. **Coffee**, too, is popular, and tastes great when **made from locally produced, freshly roasted beans**.

Thali, a synonym for variety

As a rule, you shouldn't touch anything that you can't **cook or peel**. Otherwise your holiday might be ruined by long-term gastric problems. Only drink water from bottles, and check first that the cap is really **sealed**. Even filtered water, which stands in jugs on restaurant tables, is often not pure enough for western constitutions. Buying ice cream from a beach vendor is an absolute no-no! Outside major cities, the more expensive restaurants are almost exclusively in luxury class hotels.

SHOPPING

Don't pack your suitcase to the brim otherwise it'll be overflowing for the journey home. Most holidaymakers end up having to buy an additional bag on the spot in order to get all those beautiful things back. Immerse yourself in the bustling world of markets and bazaars, but don't forget to haggle. After the trader names his price, you name yours – about half the amount. If you stick to your guns, you can usually meet somewhere in the middle. You should never respond to offers from beach vendors with a blunt 'No'. It's better to say 'maybe tomorrow'. That way there's no loss of face on either side. In the state-run emporia there are fixed prices – in contrast to the many cashmere shops, which often call themselves an emporium. Take care when purchasing antiques. There are some excellent forgers who can make furniture and coins look old. And besides you aren't allowed to take anything out of the country that's more than 100 years old.

Tailors will happily make up garments for you, such as a shirt *or a salwar kameez*, a long blouse with tapering trousers. It will take a couple of hours at most, and the price is very reasonable. The same goes for western cuts, which any Indian tailor will be able to copy for you. The shops are usually open daily.

JEWELLERY

The shops sell some beautiful gold and silver jewellery, but the gold often has a distinctive reddish tinge. Have the dealer show you a certificate of authenticity, and if you want to play safe only buy at jewellery shops that are identified as 'government approved'. Silver is very beautifully worked and often decorated with semi-precious stones. A common 'stone' is rich golden-yellow *amber*.

Glittering *bangles* have also become popular in the West – whether with stones or without, real or fake. Several are stacked on one arm, blending complimentary colours, tones and textures. In India, fashion jewellery is available everywhere from the so-called *ladies' shops*, which can often just be small kiosks.

LEATHER GOODS

Only the very elegant shopping centres, such as in Bengaluru, will sell suitcases or briefcases that conform to European tastes. Most models qualify as 'exotic' at best. That also applies to the strap sandals that are available everywhere. But there are very nice belts and wallets and all manner of etui bags.

Shop till you drop: silk, jewellery, spices –
it's one big consumer paradise at the
markets and in the bazaars and stores

PASHMINA SHAWLS

South India has lots of cashmere shops, which sell carpets, jewellery and hundreds of pashmina shawls in every imaginable colour and design. The quality varies considerably, a shawl costing anything between 43 £/56 US$ and 430 £/560 US$. Genuine shawls are made out of cashmere wool, the hair of the Himalayan mountain goat, which is five times finer than a human hair. The best quality comes from the hair under the chin of the goat, and clearly such items are going to cost a lot more than just a few pounds. As proof of the fine structure of genuine cashmere shawls, dealers will often pull them through a finger ring.

SILK AND COTTON

India's best silk comes from Mysore and Kanchipuram. It ranges from ultra fine to heavy quality. Chettinad and Madurai are well known for cotton. Even if you don't want to wear a sari yourself, the material, between 4 m/13.1 ft and 8 m/26.2 ft long and 1.2 m/3.9 ft wide, will come in handy as a sofa or bed cover, or even as a curtain. You can have pretty cushion covers made up from the broad brocade borders. Cotton comes in wonderful designs; South Indian dealers import beautiful materials in authentic colours from Gujarat, where the dyes are fixed in a salt lake.

SPICES

Saffron is one of the world's most expensive spices – but it's affordable in India, particularly in places such as the spice yards of Fort Cochin in Kerala. In the markets there are cones piled high with cardamom, ginger, turmeric, vanilla, etc.; select the amount you require and the trader will pack it for you.

GOA

In their search for spices and silk, Portuguese traders landed in Goa in 1510. They were so taken with this fertile region that they stayed for 451 years. Goa only gained independence from Portugal in 1961; in 1987 it became India's 25th state.

With colourful Hindu temples standing next to whitewashed churches, the inhabitants here have a more relaxed outlook on life than in the north. The great thing about Goa is the blend; colonial charm mixed with Indian mysticism, bustling markets and exotic fragrances. Many things here are called by their Portuguese names, and some of the older generation can still speak the language of the former colonial masters, who have also left behind their fortresses, their mansions, their food, their beliefs and their culture. With an area of 1429 mi², this is India's smallest state. At the foot of the Western Ghats mountain range, rice fields alternate with palm groves. In the settlements fringing the paddies time seems to have stood still and villages such as *Canacona taluka* near Margao appear almost untouched by civilisation.

But Goa's biggest attractions are the endless broad beaches that run the length of the 101-km/63-mi Konkan Coast, interrupted only by river estuaries. In general, the beaches in the north are livelier than those of the south. Most of them have long-since been abandoned by the hippies, who nowadays tend to congregate in the far north and far south. In the evening the lively beaches with all their activities are transformed into romantic locations, with

Shop till you drop: silk, jewellery, spices – it's one big consumer paradise at the markets and in the bazaars and stores

many restaurants setting up chairs and tables on the beach. Sitting under a starry sky, your feet in the sand and the sound of breaking waves in the background – that is the ultimate Goa experience!

CALANGUTE-BAGA

(144 A5) *(𝔐 B6)* **Once small fishing villages, the two resorts of Calangute (*koli* *gutti* = land of the fisherman) and Baga have grown together almost seamlessly (pop. 17,000).**

The double community is now a hive of activity. Calangute-Baga makes an ideal base for tours into the area north of the Mandovi River.

ST ALEX CHURCH

The two towers and dome of the snow-white St Alex Church in Calangute are visible from afar. Built more than 400 years ago, this pretty church is one of the oldest in Goa. Inside, one of the highlights is the magnificent altar. *Chogm Rd*

FOOD & DRINK

O PESCADOR RESTAURANT & BAR
This large open-air restaurant with seating for about 100 enjoys a good reputation for its fish and seafood dishes. Three times a week, there is also live music and

MACKIE'S SATURDAY NITE BAZAAR
A vibrant night market, every Saturday 6pm–midnight by the river in Baga. *www.mackiesnitebazaar.com*

SPORTS & ACTIVITIES

HOUSEBOAT TOURS
Goa offers houseboat cruises along its backwaters on a smaller scale. There are cruises of varying lengths. The 2-day tour aboard a double-decker, for example, departs Chapora/Siolim at 3pm, arriving in

Baga Beach Ball: Bend it like Beckham – or other heroes of Indian kids

karaoke. *Baga Rd, Cobra Vaddo, Calangute | tel. 098 2 21 22 21 71 | Moderate–Expensive*

SHOPPING

ALEXANDRINA BOUTIQUE
In this shop you will find the latest international fashions as well as popular Indo-ethnic mix – also tailor-made. *Baga Rd, opposite O Pescador Restaurant in the Tibetan Market, Cobra Vaddo, Calangute*

time to watch the sunset over the mangroves. *Nov–April | 132 £/170 US$ for 2 persons | Johns Boat Tours | tel. 0832 6 52 01 90 and 0703 0 55 44 00 | www.johnboattours.com*

BEACHES IN THE VICINITY

From north to south, all **(144 A5)** *(Ø B6)*

VAGATOR
This beach at the foot of Chapora Fort

consists of two sections, separated by a rocky headland. The northern part, *Ozram*, is smaller and more popular, the southern, *Big Vagator*, is more secluded. As India's first *W Hotel*, the hip *W Goa (160 rooms | tel. 0832 6718888 | www.w-goa.com | Moderate–Expensive)* was opened in 2017.

ANJUNA

Cows, ageing hippies and package tourists share the warm sands of Anjuna. At full moon, wild rave parties are held between the palm trees and the rocks.

CALANGUTE ★

The 'Queen of the Beaches' extends for more than 8 km/5 mi from Fort Aguada to the small river estuary at *Baga Beach*. Essentially, Baga, Calangute, Candolim and Sinquerim constitute different sections of what is one very long beach. The *Keys Resort Ronil (125 rooms | Baga, Sauntavaddo | tel. 0832 2276101 | www.keyshotels.com | Moderate)* designed in Portuguese style has two pools.

CANDOLIM

This busy beach is lined with shacks and bars. One nice restaurant is the *Palm & Sands (Dando | tel. 0832 2479171 | Budget)*, which serves Goan, Chinese and European cuisine. Speciality: *crème caramel*.

SINQUERIM

This narrow continuation of Candolim beach extends for 800 m/2600 ft as far as the Fort Aguada headland. Lots of water sports are on offer. Accommodation options include the colonial-style *Aldeia Santa Rita (70 rooms | Sinquerim, Candolim | tel. 0832 2 47 93 56 | www.aldeiasantarita.com | Moderate)*.

ENTERTAINMENT

TITO'S

This is a famous nightclub, dating from the hippy era. The party is still going on today. *Tito's Lane Baga | Saunto Vaddo | www.titosgroup.com*

★ **Calangute**
Thousands of palm trees line the 8-km/5-mi long 'Queen of Beaches' → p. 35

★ **Anjuna flea market**
It isn't just latter-day hippies that sell their wares here → p. 36

★ **Majorda, Colva, Benaulim, Varca**
Four beaches making up one endless palm-lined beach, with plenty of space to dream → p. 38

★ **Cavelossim, Mobor, Betul**
Peaceful, romantic, endless – just how you imagine tropical beaches → p. 38

★ **Portuguese houses in Chandor**
The Bragança House and Sara's Heritage House are living museums of the colonil era → p. 40

★ **Dona Paula**
This glorious palm-lined beach has been used as a setting for Bollywood movies → p. 41

★ **Sahakari Spice Farm**
Fragrant, spicy experience with relaxing herbal massage → p. 43

★ **Velha Goa**
The whole city has been declared a Unesco World Heritage Site → p. 43

MARCO POLO HIGHLIGHTS

WHERE TO STAY

ATMAN BEACH RESORT
RESORT ARAMBOL
Behind the sand dunes of Pernem are the resort's eco huts made from bamboo and wood, and beautifully decorated by an Italian-Indian couple. In the rooftop restaurant *Sole e Luna* they serve Italian cuisine made from regional produce. *Dando Village, Gircarwada, Arambol | Pernem | tel. 0988 1311643 | www.atmangoa.com | Budget*

CASA DE GOA
Twelve villas designed in the Mediterranean style of a boutique resort are arranged around the pool. *47 rooms | Calangute | tel. 0832 6717786 | www. casadegoa.com | Moderate–Expensive*

CASA RUTH
The guesthouse (5 mins. on foot to the beach) has four clean rooms with balconies – one with kitchenette. *7/24 B Saunta Vaddo, Baga Rd, Calangute, Bardez | tel. 0832 2277382 | Budget*

PAES PEARL BEACH VILLA
The old Goan building is 100 m/328 ft from Baga Beach. It has eight spacious rooms – ✹ four with a sea view –, two huts and four suites. *Tel. 098 2217 56 92 | Moderate*

 **YOGAMAGIC RESORT**
The eco resort under English management consists of a main building with two suites and seven tents designed in oriental style. Its situation, adjacent to a rice paddy and stream, makes it a very relaxing place, together with the yoga and Ayurveda they offer. The resort uses solar energy and recyclable materials and composts its waste. *1586/1 Grand Chinvar | Vagator, Anjuna, Bardez | tel. 0832 6523796 | www. yogamagic.net | Moderate*

INFORMATION

Only in Panjim, at the *Tourist Information Counter (tel. 0832 2 54 00 31)* at Dabolim Airport or at *www.goa-tourism.com*

WHERE TO GO

ANJUNA FLEA MARKET ★
(144 A5) (∅ B6)
In the 1970s, hippies established a flea market in St. Michael's Vaddo in South Anjuna. Today, with its stalls full of crafts from Tibet, Nepal and Kashmir, colourful clothes and tattoo artists, it is considered one of Goa's main attractions. *Oct–May | Wed 9am–6pm on Ajuna Beach*

 (144 A5) (∅ B6)
In neighbouring Arpora the bazaar really livens up on Saturday evenings. *Nov–April 6pm–after midnight*

FORT AGUADA (144 A5) (∅ B6)
Between 1609 and 1612, the Portuguese built the sprawling Fort Aguada on the headland at the end of Sinquerim beach. Within the citadel stands a white lighthouse; dating from 1846 it was the first lighthouse to be built in the whole of Asia. *6 km/3.7 mi south*

MAPUSA (144 A5) (∅ B6)
The market in Mapusa is held from Monday to Saturday. It's well worth visiting, especially on a Friday when farmers from northern Goa arrive with their fruit, vegetables, pottery, flowers and sweet bananas. *10 km/6.2 mi northeast*

PALOLEM

(144 A5) (∅ B6) **The entire *taluka* (district) of Canacona only has around**

Practical: pretty bags for carrying home pretty gifts from the Anjuna flea market

11,000 inhabitants. The lively little town of Palolem really just consists of one street, Palolem Beach Road.

It is lined with shops selling trinkets, cafés and restaurants. It is particularly popular with young travellers. Instead of smart hotels, eco resorts made of mud and bamboo are the order of the day. The half-moon beach is also known as 'Paradise Beach' – enclosed by rocky headlands and a dense palm forest. North of Palolem, Goa's finest beaches stretch as far as Majorda.

SIGHTSEEING

SRI MALLIKARJUNA TEMPLE

This temple near the small village of Sristhal in the southernmost taluka of Canacona, some 3 km/1.9 mi inland from Palolem, was built as long ago as the 16th century and is dedicated to an incarnation of Shiva. The temple contains the statues of more than 60 Hindu deities.

FOOD & DRINK

DROPADI BEACH RESTAURANT

Serving everything from lobster to lasagne to north Indian *tandoori,* this is considered one of the best restaurants in Palolem. *Palolem Beach | tel. 0832 2 64 45 55 | Moderate*

RESTAURANT SAN FRANCISCO

Located right on the beach, the open bamboo veranda is an ideal place to relax. They serve delicious and very reasonably priced Goan dishes; specialities include tiger prawns and chicken Xacuti with coconut sauce. *Palolem Beach | tel. 091 58 05 72 01 | www.campsanfrancisco.com | Budget*

SHOPPING

BUTTERFLY BOOK SHOP

Good for saving on the luggage: if you buy a book here you can sell it back to them when you've finished, naturally for a lower price. Borrowing is also possible.

Languages available range from English and German to Russian and Japanese. *Ward 14, Pundalik Gaitondi*

SPORTS & ACTIVITIES

DOLPHIN WATCHING
Many of the fishermen on Palolem Beach are happy to take tourists out for fishing excursions or to go dolphin watching.

BEACHES IN THE VICINITY

All beaches from north to south (144 A5) (*ꟿ B6*)

MAJORDA, COLVA, BENAULIM, VARCA ★
Here, to the north of Palolem, is where numerous luxury resorts are located, including the endless palm-lined beach that stretches from *Majorda* to *Varca*.

CAVELOSSIM, MOBOR, BETUL ★
This peaceful sandy beach, which has several sections, stretches north of Palolem

as far as the tip of the promontory. The 5-star resort ◑ *The Leela Goa (tel. 0832 66 21 | www.theleela.com | Expensive)* is regarded as the best hotel in the entire state. It lies between the Sal River and the peaceful Mobor Beach and has 206 rooms, six restaurants and bars, a spacious spa with Ayurveda practitioner, a 12-hole golf course and floodlit tennis courts. The complex is run sustainably using solar power and rainwater for the gardens. On the banks of the Sal River is the open-air INSIDER TIP *Fisherman's Wharf restaurant (opposite the Holiday Inn, Cavelossim, Mobor | tel. 0832 287 13 17 | thefishermanswarf.in | Moderate)*, which serves a variety of fish and seafood specialities. Also romantically situated on the Sal is the ☆ INSIDER TIP *Joe's River Cove (at the pier | Cavelossim, Mobor | tel. 098 90 02 88 18 | Budget)*, where both the seafood and the hotly spiced chicken are reasonably priced.

INSIDER TIP *AGONDA*

This 3-km/1.9-mi long natural bay is framed by palms and casuarinas and lies

On the beach of the Leela Goa resort there are still places under the palm trees

some 5 km/3.1 mi north of Palolem. The *Jardim a Mar (Agonda Beach, no. 357a, next to the church | tel. 094 20 16 24 60 | jardim-a-mar.com | Budget)* offers accommodation in 17 rooms, some in huts. They also offer yoga and Ayurveda, and from the 🍴 open-air restaurant you can watch the dolphins.

ENTERTAINMENT

PALOLEM BEACH PARTIES
The hub of local nightlife is the main Palolem beach. Every Saturday evening the British DJ Justin Mason runs his ● *Silent Noise Parties:* headphones *(600 Rs)* can be set to a variety of music styles. *10pm–4am*

WHERE TO STAY

The perfect place to unwind. This collection of 26 huts stands in a palm grove 200 m/655 ft above the south beach. The associated restaurant is mostly vegetarian. Corresponding to its holistic philosophy, this lovely little resort also offers Ayurveda and yoga as well as meditation. *296, Colomb | Palolem | tel. 0832 2 64 34 72 | www.bhaktikutir. com | Budget*

CIARAN'S CAMP ❂
Situated in verdant grounds, 37 environmentally friendly beach huts made of coir (coconut husks), either with sea or garden view. No hut is further than 20 m/65.6 ft from the beach. The library has more than 1000 titles. To save on plastic, bottles are refilled with drinking water; they also have energy-saving light bulbs. Fresh seafood is served in the open-air beach restaurant. *Palolem Beach | tel. 0832 2 64 34 77 | www.ciarans. com | Budget*

VEENIOLA HOLIDAY HOME
The cornflower blue house lies in the middle of green fields and palm groves, only a few minutes on foot from Zalor Beach. It has 14 double rooms and an amazingly good restaurant – *Por do Sol* –, well known for seafood and steaks. *Tamborim | Cavelossim | tel. 0832 2 84 47 90 | www.veeniolaholidayhome.com | Budget*

INFORMATION

Information via the *Tourist Office* in *Margao | at the railway station | Margao Residency/opposite the Municipal Council | tel. 0832 2 70 22 98*

WHERE TO GO

COTIGAO WILDLIFE SANCTUARY
(144 B6) *(ル B6)*
The 41-mi² game park lies 10 km/6 mi east of Palolem. Monkeys perform their acrobatics in the trees and, with a bit of luck, you'll be able to spot sloths, rhinos and leopards. From a 25-m/82-ft high tower you can see animals drinking at a watering hole. Best time: Oct–March. *Daily 7am–5.30pm | Range Forest Office | tel. 0832 2 96 56 01*

MARGAO (144 A5) *(ル B6)*
Goa's second-largest city (pop. 120,000) has always been an important commercial centre, particularly when it comes to agricultural produce. Especially worth seeing therefore is the market, which extends from the main square as far as the old station. In the covered labyrinth full of colours, sounds and fragrances, you will find spices, clothes, pottery and handicrafts. For a special pampering experience try the ● *Millennium Beauty Parlour (QG 7, St Anthony Complex, next to St Sebastian's Church | Aquem Alto | tel. 098 22 48 28 64).* The owner Sarita

At the Bragança estate in Chandor the daughter of the house leads you through the colonial past

Lobo does massages, manicures and pedicures, as well as facial treatments using mainly natural products. Goa's latest fashion trends are available at *Boutique Blue – Clothes Bar & A Lifestyle Store (Coelho Apartments, Shop No. 1, opposite St Sebastian's Church | Aquem Alto)*. Nelita Coelho, the owner, specialises in unusual Indo-European fusion fashion of silk, cotton, linen and chiffon with matching accessories. She also does made-to-measure garments. Crafts from all over India, made from environmentally friendly, mostly recycled materials, are available at the ⓦ *Tuk-Tuk-Shop (A 104, 1st floor, Pereira Plaza, opposite Hospicio Hospital)* and include baskets, books and writing paper processed from elephant dung. *38 km/26.3 mi north*

PORTUGUESE HOUSES IN CHANDOR ★ (144 A5) (∅ B6)

Original houses from Portuguese times, still occupied by the descendants of the people who built them, are open to visitors in Chandor. The *Bragança*

House (Mon–Sat 9am–5pm | 150 Rs) on Church Square is 450 years old in parts. Senhora Judith Borges displays the treasures of Goa's largest house: the magnificent ballroom with crystal chandeliers and typical Goan-style easy chairs. Also *Vhodlem Ghor – Fernandes Heritage Mansion (daily 9am–5.30pm | 150 Rs | Fort Area, Cotta, Chandor)* is a lively museum. The pride and joy of the Fernandes family is – apart from the ballroom – the collection of old palanquins, temple statues and 500-year-old embrasures. *38 km/26.3 mi north*

PANAJI (PANJIM)

MAP INSIDE BACK COVER
(144 A5) (∅ B6) **Goa's capital (pop. 120,000) lies on the south bank of the broad estuary of the Mandovi River. For several years the Nehru Bridge has**

linked Panaji to North Goa.
The city owes its charm to its wonderful location on the river as well as its many colonial buildings, churches, shady squares and green parks – particularly the Municipal Gardens.

SIGHTSEEING

CHURCH OF IMMACULATE CONCEPTION

Situated on the green central square of the Municipal Gardens and visible from afar is the *Church of Immaculate Conception.* There's a lovely view over Panaji from the hill, and the white Baroque church with its twin towers is the city's main landmark.

FOOD & DRINK

JOET'S GUEST HOUSE

In the open restaurants on the beach freshly caught fish and seafood are served. DJ Emmanuel also performs every Friday evening in *Joet's Guest House* with INSIDER TIP karaoke under the stars. *Bogmalo Beach 121 | tel. 0832 2538036 |* Budget

SHOPPING

The main shopping thoroughfare, *18th June Road*, runs from Church Square to Don Bosco's. Alongside the usual glamorous and glitzy sari shops, there are international designer outlets.

SPORTS AND ACTIVIES

COOKERY COURSE

For those who can't wait, Chef Branca gives Goan cookery courses – 12 noon–2pm with lunch, 5pm–7pm with dinner. *Detroit Institute | Jose Falcao Rd | tel. 098 22131835*

BEACHES IN THE VICINITY

All beaches, from north to south (144 A5) (*B6*)

DONA PAULA ★

2 km/1.2 mi to the south of Miramar this glorious beach, framed by palms and casuarinas, has often served as a setting for Bollywood movies.

INSIDER TIP BOGMALO BAY

Bogmalo Bay is shaped like a sickle. It is located 8 km/5 mi from Dabolim Airport. Because of the calm water and the gently sloping beach, bathing is safe here

LOW BUDGET

● Motorcycle pilots transport their passengers to every destination at a fraction of the cost of a taxi and will wait patiently while you see the sights. Most drivers are also knowledgeable guides. You can find them everywhere in Goa at stands marked *Two Wheeler Taxi Stand. 30 Rs/km*

Tailors have set up shop at Bogmalo Bay. Cheap and quick – they can easily copy items of clothing you bring along or will work from patterns in fashion magazines. The best in the trade are *Manolis* and *Indian Handcraft.*

Scooters, motorcycles and bicycles can be hired almost anywhere – there is no cheaper way of exploring Goa. Prices are between 250 Rs and 400 Rs per day. For scooters and motorcycles, make sure you bring along a copy of your driver's licence!

all year round. The village of the same name consists of a church, Kashmir shops and tailors.

ENTERTAINMENT

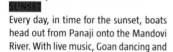

INSIDER TIP ▶ CRUISING INTO THE SUNSET

Every day, in time for the sunset, boats head out from Panaji onto the Mandovi River. With live music, Goan dancing and dinner. Booking at the quayside.

WHERE TO STAY

BOGMALLO BEACH RESORT COTTAGES
Just 300 m/984 ft from the main hotel building, ⚡ 15 beach cottages stand in their own palm tree garden, which overlooks Bogmalo Bay. All of them have a sea view and are equipped with veranda, bathroom and king-size bed. *Mormugao | tel. 0832 2 53 82 22 | www.bogmallobeachresort. com | Expensive*

CIDADE DE GOA
This luxury resort has 210 rooms, two pools and lies in park-like grounds just 7 km/4.4 mi from Panaji on the 300-m/984-ft long *Vainginim Beach.* The low-rise pink and ochre buildings have won several architectural awards. *Tel. 0832 2 45 45 45 | www.cidadedegoa. com | Expensive*

INSIDER TIP ▶ COCONUT CREEK RESORT

This magical little complex comprising ten pavilions and a pool lies hidden away in a palm grove in Bogmalo, 14 km/8.6 mi from Panaji. Bogmalo Beach is just four minutes away. The 20 large rooms all have four-poster beds. *Tel. 0832 2 53 81 00 | www.coconutcreekgoa.com | Moderate-Expensive*

DEVAAYA AND AYURVEDA & NATURE CURE CAMP
This extensive complex, with its total of 60 luxurious Goan-style rooms, nestles in lush greenery on Divar Island in the Mandovi River, so it's easy to focus on the Ayurveda treatments they have on offer. In addition: pool, tennis, badminton and yoga. *Tel. 0832 2 28 05 00 | www.devaaya.com | Moderate*

INFORMATION

GOA TOURISM DEVELOPMENT CORPORATION
2nd St, Paryatan Bhavan, Patto Center | tel. 0832 2 43 71 32 | www.goatourism. gov.in

TOURIST INFORMATION CENTER
Interstate Bus Terminus | tel. 0832 2 43 80 35, -36 | www.goakadamba.com

WHERE TO GO

GOA CHITRA ⊕ (144 A5) (𝄞 B6)
This centre (approx. 35 km/21.8 mi south) is intended to portray the entire culture of Goa. A typical village has been constructed from used materials and an organic garden created. The associated museum includes displays of handicrafts and farming equipment. There's also an open-air theatre. *Daily 9am–6pm, last admission 5pm | admission 200 Rs | St John the Baptist Church Rd, Mondo-Waddo | Benaulim | www.goachitra.co*m

MOLEM & BHAGVAN MAHAVIR WILD-LIFE SANCTUARY (144 B5) (𝄞 B6)
Goa shares this 93-mi² national park at the foot of the Western Ghats with the federal states of Maharashtra and Karnataka. The Goan part alone, the Molem National Park, covers an area

of 41 mi². The nearest town is Molem *(65 km/40.4 mi east).* Residents of the park include leopards, elephants and bison. The best views are from the 🌿 *Devil's Canyon* viewpoint, and the *Dudhsagar Falls* are truly spectacular. Jeep tours will take you into the heart of the jungle. *Daily 9.30am–5.30pm*

SAHAKARI SPICE FARM ★ ●
(144 A5) (*ɱ B6*)

This spice farm is situated near Ponda on Highway 4A, 34 km/21.1 mi southeast of Panaji. On a tour you will be able to touch and smell cloves, nutmeg, cardamom, cinnamon, ginger and vanilla. Quite touristy: the women perform a traditional folk dance as a welcome greeting. *Daily 9am–4.30pm | 500 Rs including organic lunch | National Highway (NH) 4A, Prabhu Nagar, Ponda | www.sahakarifarms.com*

SRI MANGUESH TEMPLE
(144 A5) (*ɱ B6*)

This temple stands in the small village of Priol, 28 km/17.4 mi east of Panaji. Sri Manguesh is one of the many incarnations of Shiva, and a *lingam* – a phallus stone – is dedicated to him. The most striking feature of the famous Shiva shrine is its white, seven-storey oil lamp tower.

VELHA GOA ★ (144 A5) (*ɱ B6*)

With its palaces, Baroque churches and mansions, the former capital of *Velha Goa* (pop. 5400), 10 km/6.2 mi east of Panaji, is today a Unesco World Heritage Site. Hub of Portuguese colonial power until 1759, Old Goa is a relatively peaceful place today, situated on the Mandovi River. The most famous church in Goa is the *Basilica of Bom Jesus*, which contains the relics of Saint Francis Xavier, who came to Goa as a missionary in 1542 and died in China.

Dedicated to the god Shiva, the Sri Manguesh Temple with its seven-storey oil lamp tower

KARNATAKA

Architectural jewels and historical sites wherever you roam. Magnificent palaces, richly decorated temples, mystical mosques. No Indian state has such a rich history or so many silent but also eloquent witnesses to long-lost cultures as Karnataka.

Rather than being confronted with boring, run-of-the-mill history, visible only in museums and ruins, visitors to Karnataka will experience a living past, mostly within our grasp, sometimes beyond belief. Gaze in amazement at elaborate stone reliefs depicting images of a time in which we also have our roots: reliefs festooned with figures of deities that appear to jump out of the stonework; temple dancers that seemingly gyrate to unheard melodies; erotic depictions that are enough to make the prudish blush. Nowhere else in India has such fine, vivid stone carvings as those created here in Karnataka. All these images open windows onto a world full of fairy tales and mysticism – like one enormous reference work of Indian mythology. The epitome of the fairy-tale splendour of ancient princely glory is the Maharaja's Palace in Mysore, which looks almost unworldly when illuminated at night.

As far as tourists are concerned, Karnataka does not particularly feature as a seaside destination, although it does have its fair share of fine beaches, such as the famed Om Bay, as well as a dazzling underwater world just waiting to be discovered by divers. But it's in its scenic beauty that the 73,000 mi² state comes

Ancient sites and modern cities: travel through time back to India's mythical past – and into its promising future

into its own, with a fascinating kaleidoscope of the natural world from bizarre rock formations to huge national parks full of exotic fauna and flora. Most of India's tigers survive in the game parks of Karnataka, as well as a quarter of the world's population of Asian elephants. Then there are the enchanted jungles and high mountains of the Western Ghats, which stretch for hundreds of miles through Karnataka and give trekkers and rock climbers a real treat. Spectacular waterfalls like the Jog Falls, which

in the monsoon become mighty forces of nature. And lush green tea plantations that wrap themselves around gentle hills flecked with colonial hill stations.

Karnataka also offers the most exciting contrasts. In Bengaluru, formerly Bangalore, India's own Silicon Valley, the technological future of India has well and truly begun. The city has also made a name for itself as a centre for specialist medical treatments, which work out far cheaper here than in Europe. On the other hand, it can sometimes seem as though the

The daily offering and prayers at the temple are routine even for metropolitans

wheel of time has almost come to a complete standstill, when somewhere, amid the barren, rocky landscape, an ancient ox cart emerges out of the haze.

BENGALURU (BANGALORE)

🔳 **MAP INSIDE BACK COVER**
(148 C4) (*E8–9*) With its highways and office buildings, its parks and botanical garden, this garden city (pop. 9.6 million) at a height of 949 m/3114 ft looks decidedly European. But even here the Indian past is noticeable, and there are temples and museums worth visiting. And with a temperature range of 14 to 33 degrees centigrade, it has a very pleasant climate. You can also clearly see the future that is envisaged for this IT metropolis, as it spreads out further and further, building sites all over the place.

But the eternal traffic congestion calls for strong nerves.

SIGHTSEEING

BANGALORE PALACE
The royal palace was built in 1887 and, with its turrets and towers, strongly re-

🏙 **WHERE TO START?**
Cauvery Handicraft building:
Arts and crafts are sold here, at the junction of Brigade Road and MG Road. It is not far from the *Shivaji Nagar* bus stand or the nearby underground station. From here, it is easy to reach Cubbon Park and the Lalbagh Botanical Gardens on foot. Buses go to the Tipu Sultan Palace in Old Bangalore, to the Nandi Bull Temple, Bangalore Palace and the Government Museum.

sembles Windsor Castle. Because the Maharaja still uses some of the rooms when he is in Bangalore, guided tours are by prior arrangement only. Concerts often take place in the grounds, with the likes of the Rolling Stones, Sting, Scorpions and Deep Purple having performed here over the years. *Daily 10am–5.30 pm | 460 Rs, photos 685 Rs | Palace Rd*

CUBBON PARK

Covering 320 acres, this lovely park, adorned with flowers, fountains and statues, is the green heart of the city. It is home to the state library. The *Government Museum* with its sculptures and the *Venkatappa Art Gallery (both 4 Rs)* where more than 600 paintings are on display over three floors is on Kasturba Road, close to the park. Both are open *Tue–Sun 10am–5pm.* The *Visversvarya Industrial & Technological Museum* is also on Kasturba Road *(daily 10am–5.30pm | 40 Rs).*

LALBAGH BOTANICAL GARDENS ★

Here, over an area of approx. 250 acres, you will find the largest collection of tropical and subtropical plants in India, alongside centuries-old trees. The garden was laid out in 1760. Flower shows marking India's National Holiday (26 January) and Independence Day (15 August) are organised in the glass house, which was modelled on Crystal Palace in London.; there are also folklore evenings every second Sunday. *Daily 6am–7pm | 20 Rs, free admission 6am–9am and 6pm–7pm | KH Rd | www.lalbaghgardens.com*

NANDI BULL IN THE BULL TEMPLE

The bull Nandi is the mount of the god Shiva and is worshipped accordingly. The Bull Monument in the *Bull Temple* of Bengaluru is of grey granite, almost 5 m/16.4 ft high and 6 m/19.7 ft long. The statue is polished daily and decorated with garlands. *Bull Temple Rd, Basavanagudi*

MARCO POLO HIGHLIGHTS

★ **Lalbagh Botanical Gardens**
A floral oasis in the heart of the city with a fragrant rose garden and Art Deco greenhouse → **p. 47**

★ **Golden Chariot**
The journey is just as good as the destination, aboard this luxury train → **p. 50**

★ **Hampi**
A simply magical, riverside location: an ancient temple among the rocks → **p. 50**

★ **Cave temples**
In the sacred caves of Badami, Lord Shiva has 81 dance variations → **p. 55**

★ **Gol Gumbaz**
Echoes repeat eleven times in the whispering gallery of this enormous mausoleum in Bijapur → **p. 55**

★ **Chennakesava Temple**
Study the thousands of figures from long-lost cultures on the temple façade → **p. 58**

★ **Om Beach**
Gokarna: a beach with symbolism → **p. 59**

★ **Shravanabelagola**
Gigantic: the statue of Lord Gomateswara is 17 m/55.8 ft high → **p. 60**

★ **Mysore Palace**
Like a fairy-tale from "One Thousand and One Nights" → **p. 61**

★ **Nagarhole National Park**
Close encounters with tigers and elephants → **p. 63**

FOOD & DRINK

BLUE GINGER IN THE TAJ WEST END
Authentic Vietnamese dishes, prepared by chef Doung, are prepared under an open thatched roof in the middle of a tropical garden. Guests travelling alone are given two ● INSIDER TIP ▶ goldfish in a bowl on the table for company. Next door is *The Blue Bar,* one of the city's fashionable nightspots. *Taj West End | 25 Racecourse Rd | tel. 080 66 60 56 60 | www.tajhotels.com | Expensive*

MR BEANS – THE COFFEE LOUNGE
Those who can't do without their Italian coffee routine complete with latte macchiato, espresso, cappuccino and 30 different types of iced coffee have come to the right place in this smart white villa. The finest Indian tea is also served here, and in the stylish ambience the various fruit flavours of a shisha also taste good. *651 Tank Rd, Koramangala | tel. 080 41 11 57 17 | www.mrbeans.in | Moderate*

MTR (MAVALLI TIFFIN ROOMS)
Tiffin means snack, and that is the speciality of MTR, Bengaluru's oldest vegetarian restaurant. But breakfasts, lunch and evening meals are also served. You should definitely give the *idlis* a try – delicious little pancakes made of rice and semolina with a spicy sauce. Dark furniture helps to retain the atmosphere of the 1920s. *14 Lalbagh Rd, near the Botanical Gardens | tel. 080 22 22 00 22 | www.mavallitiffinrooms.com | Budget*

ULLA'S REFRESHMENTS
From the ☼ terrace on the first floor you can enjoy a great view over the bustle of MG Road. The vegetarian dishes here can be taken as snacks or as complete meals. *MG Rd, Public Utility Bldg | tel. 080 25 58 74 86 | Moderate*

SHOPPING

BANDHEJ
Fantastic quality and unique patterns at reasonable prices! The Bandhej store chain stands for modern designs with a 'touch of India'. All textiles are created, produced and hand-embroidered in the in-house studio, or decorated with block prints. *503 CMH Rd, opposite Max Muller Bhavan | www.bandhej.com*

CENTRAL COTTAGE INDUSTRIES EMPORIUM
The store is managed by the Ministry of Textiles. In addition to fabrics there are also hand-produced art objects, jewellery and fashion accessories created by artists and skilled artisans. Everything is available at fixed prices. *144 MG Rd, Shubharam Complex | www.thecottage.in*

INSIDER TIP ▶ GANGARAM'S BOOK BUREAU

Bookworms are sure to find what they're looking for amongst the thousands of titles spread across three floors. The friendly staff will look out a required volume on request. The shop, with its many reading corners, has been around for more than 30 years. *48 Church St, 2nd floor, Triumph Tower*

ENTERTAINMENT

Bengaluru has the large international business contingent to thank for its high density of pubs and bars. In the pubs, alcohol can only be served until 11.30pm

HARD ROCK CAFÉ
The huge cult café is divided up into three different areas – a restaurant with seating for 100, a bar and an open courtyard, as well as a Rock Shop. Like Hard Rock Cafés all over the world, this one is deco-

rated with memorabilia and collectibles from rock greats. With a bit of luck you might see a jam session going on. *40 St Marks Rd*

LOCK N LOAD PUB

This mixture of pub, disco and bar in the Chairman's Resort is one of Bangalore's Top Ten. Everything is done in Wild West style, from old comic-book images and waiters dressed in cowboy clothes to a huge dance floor with constantly changing, coloured light reflections and saddles as chairs. There's an in-house DJ to look after the sound. *Closed Sun | No. 14/1 Kodigehalli Main Rd, Sahakar Nagar, Hebbal, near the Twin Towers | www.chairmansresort.com*

SHIRO

After Mumbai and Goa, Shiro has now taken Bangalore by storm as the place for fine dining. There is opulence on all three levels of this restaurant/lounge complex: statues of Greek gods, fountains, Buddha statues and a DJ console set in the 'sky'. And right at the top is Bangalore's largest

roof terrace. The menu offers a range of Japanese, Chinese, Korean and Thai specialities like sushi, sashimi, dim sum, plus more than 20 vegetarian dishes. *UB City (large shopping centre), 24 Vittal Mallya Rd | www.shiro.co.in*

WHERE TO STAY

INSIDER TIP OUR NATIVE VILLAGE

This village lies an hour away from Bangalore and offers, in contrast to the hi-tech city, a holiday on a farm – ideal for families with kids. You can milk the cows, drive an ox-cart, fly kites, go cycling and learn about organic farming. There's even a spa with holistic treatments. *Kodihalli Village, Hessarghatta Rd | tel. 080 4114 09 09 | www.ournativevillage.com | Moderate*

ST MARK'S HOTEL

The 4-star boutique hotel has a good location on one of the town's main streets. The marble lobby and 96 rooms with free WiFi have cool interiors with a touch of India. There is a fitness centre and a styl-

Shopping, the popular pastime for many global city-slickers, ist particularly rewarding in Bengaluru

ish, white roof-top garden. *4/1 St Mark's Rd | Tel. 080 22 27 90 90 | www.stmarks hotel.com | Moderate*

TAJ WEST END

An oasis of peace with excellent service, whose former patrons include Winston Churchill, Queen Elizabeth II and Queen Silvia of Sweden. Breakfast can be served under the massive 150-year-old rain tree on request. It takes 45 minutes to follow the nature trail through the extensive grounds. In addition, there are two outdoor pools, tennis courts, a spa and *Bangalore Golf Club* (18-hole) right next door. *91 rooms, 26 suites | Race Course Rd | tel. 080 66 60 56 60 | www.tajhotels. com | Expensive*

WOODLANDS

This large hotel with its 211 rooms, some of them in cottages, was one of the first in Bangalore and it exudes a nostalgic charm. Facilities include a pool and a small beauty salon. *Raja Rammohan Roy Rd | tel. 099 02 09 11 11 | www.woodlands. in | Budget–Moderate*

INFORMATION

KARNATAKA STATE TOURISM DEVELOPMENT CORPORATION
49 Khanija Bhavan | Race Course Rd | tel. 080 22 35 29 01 | www.karnataka holidays.net

KSTDC CENTRAL RESERVATION COUNTER
Badami House, N.R. Square | Tel. 080 22 27 58 69

WHERE TO GO

GOLDEN CHARIOT ★
The luxury train decorated in the style of historic maharajas' trains is the most stylish mode of transport for travelling across Karnataka. It also offers a restaurant and bar, like in 1001 Nights, with modern facilities like the Ayurveda wellness, fitness and business coach. From Bengaluru the Golden Chariot stops at Karnataka's most beautiful destinations on a journey lasting seven days: Mysore, Nagarhole Tiger Reserve, Shravanabelagola, Belur and Halebid, Hampi, Badami and Pattadakal. Finally, there is also a day's bathing in Goa. *7 nights 4220 £/5530 US$ | Booking in Europe: The Indian Experience | tel. 0044 1865 5 55 42 77 | www.goldenchariot.org*

INSIDER TIP PUTTAPARTHI
(148 C2) *(∅ F7)*
Just 160 km/100 mi north of Bengaluru, in the neighbouring state of Andra Pradesh, lies the ashram of the spiritual master Sri Sathya Sai Baba *(www.sathyasai.info)*, who died in 2011. Followers from all over the world still flock to *Prashanti Nilayam*, the 'Abode of Highest Peace'. Accommodation at the ashram, which costs only a few rupees, cannot be booked in advance; the *accommodation office* allocates rooms from 8am onwards. Apart from the ashram, there are plenty of hotels in Puttaparthi, such as *Sri Sai Sadan Guest House (36 rooms | near the Venugopal Swamy Temple | tel. 08555 28 75 07 | Budget)* or *Hotel Sai Towers (27 rooms | Main Rd | tel. 08555 28 72 70 | www.saitowers.com | Moderate)*. There's a train from Bangalore to Puttaparthi or you can take a taxi from the new airport *(approx. 2 hours | from about 35 £/45 US$)*.

HAMPI

(145 E5) *(∅ D6)* **This is surely one of the most unusual and intriguing places**

in all India. ★ **Hampi was the capital of the Vijayanagar Empire, a kingdom that once covered the whole of South India and stretched as far as Sri Lanka.**
For more than 200 years (1336–1565), Hampi was a thriving city. At its height it would have had a population of some 500,000 – the present-day village of Hampi has only around 1500 inhabitants. But it's still possible to imagine the city's former splendour; in 1986, it was declared a Unesco World Heritage Site. As well as scattered ruins, within a radius of 26 km/16 mi among the bizarre granite rocks south of the Tungabhadra River, lie some well-preserved temples and other impressive buildings.

SIGHTSEEING

The best way to explore the extensive area of the ruined city is on a bike. Temples and monuments are open daily 8.30am–5.30pm. In 2013, the street with bazaars was cleared and rebuilt about 4 km/2.5 mi behind Kaddirampur.

Combined admission to Vittala Temple, Lotus Mahal, elephant stables and museum 500 Rs, video 25 Rs

QUEEN'S BATHROOM
The exterior is less impressive, but the interior compensates with its amazing stucco decoration, vaulted corridor and airy balconies protruding over a 15 m × 15 m/50 × 50 ft pool. Perfumed water from the lotus-shaped fountains splashed on to the ladies of the court.

ELEPHANT STABLES
An impressive building with numerous domed ceilings that once housed the royal elephants.

HAZARA RAMA TEMPLE
This royal temple is decorated all over with bas-reliefs, which depict scenes from the Hindu epic, the Ramayana.

ROYAL PALACE
In the largest section is a platform with lively bas-reliefs whose themes include

Out of this world? Hampi's bizarre mix of temples and surrounding granite rocks

hunting, dancing and processions. Just over 100 m/328 ft to the west of that was the audience chamber of the king, complete with pool.

LOTOS MAHAL

The yellow building consists of open pavilions on the ground floor and balconies on the upper floor. The architecture is an impressive example of a successful fusion of Hindu and Islamic elements. The name of the building

VITTALA TEMPLE

Dating from the 16th century, this well-preserved temple lies some 2 km/ 1.2 mi from the bazaar, Hampi's market, which borders the historic site. In the temple courtyard is the most photographed sight in all of South India: the so-called Stone Chariot, whose wheels once even turned. The outer pillars of the temple are known as the 'Musical Pillars' as they echo when banged. Vittala Temple is considered the pinnacle

Top parking spot: the Stone Chariot has been stationary in the courtyard of the Vittala Temple for around 500 years

comes from the beautiful and geometrically arranged arches, which resemble the petals of a lotus flower. *250 Rs, camera 50 Rs, video 50 Rs*

VIRUPAKSHA TEMPLE

The temple is dedicated to Lord Shiva and is still used by devout Hindus today. Visible from afar is the nine-storey *gopuram*, entrance tower. If you buy a basket of offerings with flowers and fruit *(30–50 Rs)*, take care, because the cheeky monkeys are just waiting to snatch it from you. *Camera 50 Rs, video 500 Rs*

of Vijayanagar art *(200 Rs; the ticket is also valid for admission to the Zenana complex with the Lotos Mahal and the Elephant Stables)*.

FOOD & DRINK

There are numerous small restaurants all around the Hampi bazaar.

INSIDER TIP GOPI GUEST HOUSE

You have a wonderful view of everything from the ☀ roof-top terrace of this restaurant: the river and Virupaksha temple.

It's particularly magical in the evenings! Indian and European dishes are available, such as pizza. *Janatha Plot | tel. 094 48 76 52 13 | www.gopi-guesthouse.com | Budget–Moderate*

MANGO TREE

The position of this popular restaurant was sacrificed for the redevelopment of Hampi. The garden has disappeared – along with the mango tree. But the exotic flair remains with seating for 60 guests (floor and tables), and delicious food – also vegetarian options. *River Side Drive, near Virupaksha Temple | tel. 094 48 76 52 13 | Budget*

SPORTS & ACTIVITIES

MOPED HIRE

A moped or scooter is a good way of exploring Hampi. Moped shops can be found in the area of the Hampi bazaar, in Kamalapura and in Hospet *(from approx. 150 Rs per day)*.

FUN AND GAMES AFTER THE RICE HARVEST ●

After the rice harvest, between December and March, the farmers around Hampi finally have the time to relax – enjoying ox-cart racing and the local, harmless version of bullfighting, when the toreros have to capture sweets or money that have been fixed to the animal's head. Other entertainment includes village games with coconuts and also chicken fights(!). Visitors are welcome to join in. Information: *Tourist Information Office Hampi | Hampi Bazaar | tel. 08394 24 13 39*

WHERE TO STAY

In Hampi itself there's plenty of accommodation, but it's all of the basic variety. Those looking for greater comfort are better off heading for Hospet, 13 km/8.1 mi away.

HOTEL MALLIGI

With 160 rooms, this is the best hotel in Hospet. It has four restaurants, a lovely pool, spa and fitness centre. *6/143 J. N. Rd | tel. 08394 22 81 01 | www.malligi hotels.com | Moderate*

SHANTI GUEST HOUSE

This charming establishment has 23 rooms, each with a ceiling fan, plus a lush garden overlooking the river, hammocks and bicycles. In the attached restaurant, everything from Nepalese to Thai and Israeli cuisine is served. The atmosphere is friendly and personal. *On*

LOW BUDGET

Much cheaper than taxis: comfortable, air-conditioned Volvo buses leave every 30 minutes from various points in the city from 250 Rs to *Kempegowda International Airport (KIAL),* which lies 38 km/24 mi outside the centre. *Bangalore Metropolitan Transport Corporation (BMTC), Airport Kiosk Information | tel. 077 60 99 12 69; Kempegowda Bus Station Majestic | tel. 080 22 38 58 48; Shivajinagar Bus Stand | tel. 080 22 86 16 84*

A bed will only cost a few rupees at the station in Bijapur *(Railway Retiring Room and Dorm).* The accommodation is very clean. Ask the supervisor at the station. The same applies to many Indian stations and airports, the latter with dormitories mostly in the *Domestic Terminal.*

the other side of the river, *Virupapur Gaddi, Sanapur | tel. 08394 32 53 52 | www.shanthihampi.com | Budget*

SHIVANANDA
The 23 rooms are simple but clean. While it doesn't have its own restaurant (food can be ordered in), it does have an in-house astrologer. *College Rd, next to the bus stop | tel. 094 49 23 37 66 | Moderate*

INFORMATION

TOURIST INFORMATION OFFICE HAMPI
Next to Lotus Mahal | tel. 08394 24 13 39. They also arrange personal guides, for one day *(500 Rs)* or half-day *(300 Rs)*.

WHERE TO GO

AIHOLE (145 D4) *(ₐ D5)*
With around 140 temples, Aihole is the cradle of Indian sacred architecture. The oldest building is thought to be the Lad Khan Temple, dating from the 5th–7th century, with its semi-circular apse. It stands on a raised plinth, and the entire sanctuary is surrounded by a gallery of carvings.

Most of the temples here are dedicated to the Lord Vishnu. Half of them lie within the perimeter wall *(daily 6am–6pm | 200 Rs, video 25 Rs)*. Accommodation is best found in Badami *(44 km/27.3 mi southwest of Aihole)*, and the tourist office responsible for Aihole *(in the Hotel Mayura Chalukya, Ramdurga Rd | tel. 08357 22 00 46)* is also there. *144 km /89.5 mi) northwest*

BADAMI (145 D4) *(ₐ D6)*
This beautifully situated little town (pop. 31,000), around 100 km/62 mi from Hampi, is bordered to the east by

FOR BOOKWORMS AND FILM BUFFS

The God of Small Things – Arundhati Roy tells the story of a family in Kerala, which is torn apart by forbidden love. At the same time, the author depicts the simple life of rural India in all its different guises. Brilliant!

Plain Tales from the Hills – A highly amusing classic by Bombay-born Rudyard Kipling, who provides an entertaining insight into the mundane and often decadent lives of British sahibs and memsahibs in the hill stations.

Best Exotic Marigold Hotel – This 2012 film with its all-star cast (Judi Dench, Maggie Smith, Bill Nighy) transports the audience into the bustling melee of modern-day India. For a variety of reasons, seven English pensioners converge on this hotel, which promises absolute nirvana. The reality is rather different. With a strong dash of British humour, director John Madden weaves a fine web of interpersonal relationships in an alien world.

Monsoon Wedding – This lavish production (2001) directed by Mira Nair uses a wedding to highlight the conflicts between Indian immigrants to America and the older generation back home. At the same time, it captures the wild elation of Indians during the monsoon season, with all the colour and typical Bollywood music and dance routines.

You can take dance classes in the cave temple – from Lord Shiva in person

Agastyatirtha Lake, which is surrounded by rugged, red sandstone outcrops. The dynasty of the early western Chalukya made Badami its capital and, from the end of the 6th century until the 8th century, created important sacred caves and temples here. Cut into the rock and reached via steps are four old ★ *cave temples (daily 6am–6pm | 200 Rs, video 25 Rs)*, whose entrance is marked by columns and brackets. The largest one is Cave 3, which is dedicated to the Lord Vishnu. A particularly eye-catching feature in Cave 1 is the 18-armed Nataraja (Shiva), which depicts 81 different dance moves. A view over the various temples and ruins of the North Fort is only possible by climbing up a steep flight of steps. Slightly outside the town centre is the very peaceful *Krishna Heritage (tel. 08357 22 13 00 | www.krishnaheritage badami.com | Moderate)* – 16 Villas with rooms measuring 269 ft² and outdoor showers in an attractive flower garden about 2.5 acres. It also offers fitness facilities with pool and Ayurveda spa. Or there's the *KSTDC Hotel Mayura Chaluk-*ya *(25 rooms | Ramdurg Rd | tel. 08357 22 00 46 | Moderate)*, a state-run establishment in a peaceful location some distance outside the town centre. It also runs the *Tourist Office*.

BIJAPUR (145 D3) *(ꝏ D5)*
The former capital (pop. 326,000) of the Adil Shahi kings (1489–1686) reflects the power and influence of the Muslim sultans. It is full of mosques, palaces, forts, towers and a monumental mausoleum. The latter, the ★ *Gol Gumbaz (daily 6.30am–5.30pm | 200 Rs, video camera 25 Rs),* was erected in 1659 and is the most famous building in the city. It is crowned by one of the largest domes in the world – supported by an amazing system of interlocking pendentives. Beneath the dome runs the circular 'whispering gallery', which rebounds an echo eleven times from any given position. Because of the noise levels generated by lots of visitors, it's recommended to come here early in the morning. The Palace Mosque of Ibrahim Rauza with its mausloeum lies outside the city walls.

The tomb was built by Sultan Ibrahim Adil Shah (1580–1627), and contains the graves of the ruler and his wife, Taj Sultana.

The same applies for the *mosque (daily 6am–6pm | 200 Rs, video 25 Rs)*. With its four minarets, it is thought to have served as the model for the Taj Mahal in Agra.

A good vegetarian restaurant with pleasant atmosphere is *The Chervil (Parekh Signature Mall, 1st floor. | Lingadgudi Rd | tel. 098445 8 56 77 | Moderate)* that

JOG FALLS ● (147 D2) (*ØØ C7*)

The second-highest waterfall in Karnataka (199 km/124 mi north), which plunges 253 m/830 ft into the depths from the 200-m/656-ft wide bed of the Sharavati River, is undoubtedly the most impressive, primarily because it consists of just one solid column of water that cascades into the gorge over four distinct levels. It's possible to bathe at the base of the falls. For the best views try ⋙ *Watkin's Platform* or the ⋙ *cliffs* by the *Bombay Bungalow*.

The Jog Falls plunge spectacularly into the depths. It's possible to swim at the base of the falls

is built around a patio and near to Gol Gumpaz and the train station. Accommodation is provided by the *Hotel Madhuvan (36 rooms | Station Rd | tel. 08352 25 55 71 | Moderate)*, complete with garden restaurant, lovely courtyard and fantastic view of the Gol Gumbaz from the ⋙ roof terrace. Or the *Sanman (24 rooms | Station Rd, opposite the Gol Gumbaz | tel. 08352 25 18 66 | Budget)*, which offers good value for money. The *Tourist Office (on Station Rd | tel. 08352 25 04 01)* lies behind the hotel *Mayura Adil Shahi. 160 km/99 mi northwest*

Accommodation: *Stay@Matthuga (Talavata, BH Rd (NH 206) | tel. 09880 9 99 75 | www.matthuga.in | Budget)*, 8 km/5 mi from the falls, in the middle of an areca plantation (betel nut palms).

PATTADAKAL (145 D4) (*ØØ D5*)

This Unesco World Heritage Site lies 122 km/76 mi from Hampi 22 km/13.7 mi northeast of Badami) on the Malaprabha River, and its monuments demonstrate just how varied Chalukya architecture was. Pattadakal's ten temples are among the most important early stone temples in India. The largest is the *Virupaksha Temple.* It has an enormous entrance, whose massive columns are decorated with reliefs depicting scenes from the two Hindu epics, Ramayana and Mahabharata. Opposite the temple stands a pavilion with an enormous Nandi bull. The *Mallikarjuna Temple* is similar in design, only a little smaller. The *Papanatha Temple* is a further showpiece, with finely chiselled ceilings and a hall of 16 columns. It's best to stay overnight in Badami. *Daily 6am–6pm | 500 Rs, video 25 Rs.* Information: *Tourist Office Badami in the Hotel Mayura Chalukya, Ramdurga Rd | tel. 08357 22 04 04*

MANGALURU (MANGALORE)

(147 E4) *(Ⓜ C9)* **So far the west coast of Karnataka has remained relatively undiscovered. In this hilly city (pop. 900,000) at the confluence of Gurupura and Nethravathi rivers, something of its heyday as a major port and shipbuilding centre still lingers.**

Today, from the new port, 10 km/6.2 mi north of the city centre, they export mainly coffee, pepper and cashew nuts. Along the narrow, often palm-lined streets stand old houses with roofs of red tile. After waves of conquest and destruction, not much is left in terms of important sights, nevertheless Mangalore makes an excellent base for some interesting excursions.

KADRI MANJUNATHA TEMPLE
This temple lies some 3 km/1.9 mi from the city centre and is thought to be almost 1000 years old. Devotees come here to worship a large *lingam* (stone phallus as a symbol of Shiva) and a 1.6-m/5.2-ft high bronze statue of the goddess Lokeshwara with three faces and six arms. The latter is regarded as one of the finest bronze statues in India. At 8am, noon and 8pm INSIDER TIP blessings with fire.

MANGALADEVI TEMPLE
With a dark-red tiled roof dating from the 10th century, this low-rise temple was named after the Malabar princess Mangala Devi, the patron deity of Mangalore. It is said that whoever worships at her statue will be blessed with good fortune and prosperity. Its full name is the Mahatobhara Sri Mangaladevi Temple and it is situated in Bolar, 3 km/1.9 mi southwest of the city.

ST ALOYSIUS COLLEGE CHAPEL
This fine chapel is situated in the heart of the city on Lighthouse Hill. It is visited primarily for its impressive wall and ceiling frescoes that were painted in the late 19th century by the Jesuit priest Antonio Moscheni. They depict biblical scenes, including the Apostle Thomas, who is said to have introduced Christianity to India. *Mon–Sat 8.30am–6pm, Sun 10am–noon, 2pm–6pm*

FOOD & DRINK

DIESEL CAFÉ
Bright and cheerful, with a friendly atmosphere, serving a mix of Italian and Indian dishes. The breakfast servings are particularly lavish. *Collectors Gate, Balmatta Rd | tel. 0824 2 41 06 01 | Budget*

LALITH
This restaurant might be in the basement but it offers an excellent choice of fish and seafood, cold beer and friendly service. *Balmatta Rd | tel. 0824 2 42 67 93 | Budget–Moderate*

SHOPPING

CAUVERY KARNATAKA ARTS & CRAFTS

In this state-run arts and crafts emporium, the prices for material and items such as statues made of sandalwood and bronze are fixed. *Raj Towers | Balmatta Rd*

BEACHES

INSIDER TIP *Ullal Beach*, a sandy beach 8 km/5 mi outside Mangalore, is bordered by the south bank of the Netravati River and is lined with casuarina trees.

ENTERTAINMENT

CAFÉ MOJO

The English writer George Orwell once raved about Café Mojo. After Goa, the concept of pub and bistro with dancing was also adopted at the *Goldfinch Hotel* in Mangalore. The retro-look has been kept with seating for 65 guests – also in a separate smokers' area. Guests purchase a voucher worth 1000 Rs which is used for everything. *Daily from 11.30am | Bunts Hostel Rd | cafemojo.in*

WHERE TO STAY

THE GATEWAY HOTEL ☆

From this modern 4-star establishment with its 88 bright rooms you can have a lovely view over the fishing port. The hotel has a pool and fitness centre. *Old Port Rd | tel. 0824 6 66 04 20 | www.thegatewayhotels.com | Moderate*

INSIDER TIP SUMMER SANDS BEACH RESORT

Due to its location, this idyllic beach resort is much appreciated by artists and creative types. Huts with tiled roofs housing a total of 75 rooms are dotted around the garden, which has more than 500 palm trees. You can even watch dolphins frolicking from the beach. The hotel also has a pool and rents out bicycles for exploration of the numerous lagoons in the vicinity. *Chotamangalore, Ullal | tel. 0824 2 46 76 90 | www.summersands.in | Moderate–Expensive*

HOTEL SURYA

The 18 rooms are nothing special, but this budget hotel does have a quiet location away from the street. *Greens Compound | Balmatta Rd | tel. 0824 2 42 57 36 | Budget*

INFORMATION

KARNATAKA TOURISM INFORMATION CENTER

KMC Mercana Trunk Rd | tel. 0824 2 45 39 26

KSTDC BOOKING

Corporation Commercial Block, 1st block, Lalbagh | tel. 0824 2 45 18 88

WHERE TO GO

BELUR (147 F4) (𝄞 D8)

Belur is famous for the magnificent Hoysala Temple complex. The Hoysala Empire ruled most of the modern-day state of Karnataka between 1040 and 1345. On the site the biggest attraction is the ★ *Chennakesava Temple*, which King Vishnuvardhana had built in 1117 to commemorate his victory over the Cholas. Its facade is richly decorated with life-like sculptures of musicians, dancers and erotic figures. Surrounding the plinth are 644 elephants, each one different from the next. *Daily 7.30am–7pm. 165 km/103 mi) northeast*

GOKARNA (147 D2) (𝄞 B7)

Most travellers visit this pilgrimage destination not for the temple but for the legendary ★ *Om Beach*. The beach acquired its name because its curving bays and headlands which create a shape reminiscent of the sacred Om symbol of Hindus and Buddhists. It is followed by another

109 mi) northeast of Mangalore. Here it's worth taking a look at the *Hoysaleswara Temple*, whose walls are richly decorated with a variety of Hindu deities, stylised animals and scenes from the lives of the Hoysala kings.

Shoes off, sand between your toes, relaxed conversations – end of the day at Ullal Beach

four sandy bays: *Gokarna, Kudle, Half Moon* and *Paradise*. The Kudle Beach View Resort & Spa (Kudle Beach Rd | tel. 081 30 96 76 66 | kudlebeachview.com | *Budget*) is located on the cliff, with 16 rooms, a pleasant garden, a restaurant on the rooftop terrace and pool. The ● 🐾 *Swaswara* (Dhonibail, Om Beach, Gokarna | tel. 08386 25 71 32 | www.swaswara.com | *Expensive*) has 27 villas with spacious rooms and a yoga deck; other facilities include an Ayurveda centre and large pool. Recycling is also popular – organic products are on offer and local traders are used. In the *Namasté Café* (*Budget*) at Om Beach you can get continental food, such as pizza and pasta, as well as falafel. Information: tel. 0948 31 22 33 | www.namastego karna.com. 185 km/115 mi north.

HALEBID (147 F3) *(Ø D8)*
The old Hoysala capital lies 176 km/

HASSAN (147 F4) *(Ø D8)*
This rather austere town makes a good starting point for visiting nearby Belur, Halebid and Shravanabelagola. Many tourists on this circuit stay at the pleasant garden complex of *Hoysala Village Resort* (Belur Rd | tel. 08172 25 67 95 | *Expensive*), that lies 6 km/3.7 mi) from Hassan in the direction of Belur and offers 49 rooms in cottages, as well as a pool and spa. Another option is the modern *Hassan Ashok* (BM Rd | tel. 08172 26 87 31 | www.has sanashok.com | *Moderate*), which has 36 rooms with rattan furniture, is very well maintained and offers excellent cuisine. Information: *Tourist Office | A.V.K. College Rd | tel. 08172 26 88 62. 160 km/99 mi east*

MURUDESHWAR (147 D2) *(Ø B7)*
For one of the best dive sites in South India, travel north along the coast from Mangalore for about 150 km/93 mi.

From *Murudeshwar* near Bhatkal, there's great diving and snorkelling in the amazing underwater world (wrecks included) off the small island of INSIDER TIP *Netrani (Pigeon Island)*. Contact PADI certified Netrani Adventures | 5000 Rs per dive, 1850 Rs for snorkelling | tel. 09900 55 44 22 | www.netraniadventures.com

SHRAVANABELAGOLA ★
(148 A4) (ᗝ D9)

This important place of pilgrimage for the Jains is located 125 km/78 mi east of Mangalore. At Shravanabelagola stands the colossal, monolithic statue of Lord Gomateswara, a Jain deity. The 17-m/55.8-ft high, naked figure carved from granite, with its extra long arms symbolising wisdom, can be seen from up to 30 km/18.6 mi away. To get to the top of Vindhyagiri Hill you can either climb the 614 steps or have yourself carried up in a litter. Every twelve years (the last time was in 2005), ceremonies lasting several days are performed in honour of Lord Gomateswara. *Free admission, donations welcome.* Information: *Tourist Office | at the foot of Vindhyagiri Hill | tel. 08176 25 72 54*

MYSORE

(148 A5) (ᗝ D9) **This former capital of the princely state (pop. 1 million) has a majestic aura. Here the pace is much more relaxed than in Bengaluru.**

There's something magical about the broad, tree-lined avenues, villas with pink bougainvillea spilling from their gardens and the parks surrounding the shining white *Lalith Mahal Palace* – today a hotel. Even if the many souvenir shops and bland new-builds rather dull the image, in the evening, when the sun no longer illuminates the facades so mercilessly, Mysore suddenly basks again in its ageless beauty.

SIGHTSEEING

CHAMUNDI HILL ☼
Some 1000 steps lead to the top of this 1062-m/3484-ft high hill, which is

ELEPHANT TOURISM

Tourists and elephants in Asia – it's a tricky subject. Be it in Thailand, Vietnam or South India – interaction with the domesticated elephants is usually highly commercialised and a lucrative business. Elephant camps are abundant, with a variety of offers from merely interacting with the animals, such as feeding and stroking, to shows with "painting" elephants and ride tours with heavy seats as well as Mahout (trainer) courses lasting several days with the "elephant driver's licence". The line is continually blurred between sanctuary or retirement home for older "jumbos" and enterprising business to entertain tourists. It is advisable to avoid all circus programmes with show artistry that may be unkind for the elephants. A new trend is obvious: the first tour operators are cancelling offers, which include visits to shows, when the elephants provide entertainment. See for yourself how the animals look on the spot, or plan ahead and find out more facts from the local animal welfare organisations.

crowned by the Sri Chamundeswari Temple with its richly decorated *gopuram* (entrance tower). A little further down stands the 4.8-m/15.7-ft high Nandi Bull, which was hewn out of black granite in 1659.

JAYACHAMARAJENDRA ART GALLERY
This gallery contains precious treasures of the maharajas, including antique furniture, old musical instruments and figures of ivory and sandalwood. It is housed in the Jagan Mohan Palace, west of the enormous Maharaja's Palace. *Daily 8.30am–5pm | 120 Rs*

MYSORE PALACE ★
The focal point of the city is the magnificent Maharaja's Palace *(Amba Vilas)*, built in Indo-Sarenic style and richly adorned with domes, towers, arches and colonnades. It was built in 1912 to replace the previous palace from 1897 that had burned down, and is a treasure trove of exquisite carvings, works of art from around the world, old paintings and a throne of pure gold. On Sundays and public holidays the palace is illuminated from 7pm–7.45pm by 96,000 light bulbs. *Daily 10am–5.30pm | 200 Rs | admission through the south gateway, Purandara Dasa Rd | www.mysorepalace.gov.in*

At their destination: pilgrims in front of Lord Gomateswara

Siddharta | Guest House Rd | tel. 0821 2 52 28 88 | Budget

PARK LANE HOTEL
On Saturdays, there is a pool-side barbeque at this hotel. Otherwise, it is a romantic spot for dinner. *2720 Harska Rd | tel. 0821 4 00 35 00 | www.parklane mysore.com | Expensive*

FOOD & DRINK

EDELWEISS
Café serving Austrian specialities. The kitchen is open so guests can watch as their schnitzel, etc, is being prepared. They also serve really good coffee. *2681/1 9th Cross, Adipampa Rd, V.V. Mohalla | tel. 0821 6 45 24 48 | Moderate*

OM SHANTI
In addition to serving dishes from all over the world, the speciality of this restaurant is its cheap but tasty *thalis. Hotel*

SHOPPING

Mysore is famous for its extravagant silks, sandalwood, rosewood carvings and wooden toys, as well as its pictures using natural colours and gold leaf depicting scenes from Hindu mythology.

CAUVERY ARTS & CRAFTS EMPORIUM
Artisan crafts and many items made from sandalwood; there is also genuine sandalwood powder here. High-quality products made from brass and the well-known Mysore pictures are available.

Fixed prices. *Sayyaji Rao Rd | www.cau veryhandicrafts.net*

INSIDER TIP DEVARAJA FRUIT & VEGETABLE MARKET ●

This wonderful market appeals to all the senses in equal measure. In the fruit hall there's the sweet smell of mangos and bananas, while in the flower hall you'll be almost overwhelmed by the fragrance of thousands of jasmine flowers and roses. A visual feast is provided by the tall, conical mounds of coloured powder *(kumkum)*. *Daily 6am–8.30pm | Sayyaji Rao Rd*

KSIC GOVERNMENT SILK FACTORY

Mysore is renowned for its beautiful silk. You can go right to the source, to a factory, and watch weavers as they produce the finest silk saris with ornamental trims. In the shop, apart from saris, you can buy precious fabrics in every imaginable colour and pattern, by the metre and at factory prices. *Mananthody Rd | www.ksicsilk.comc*

SANDALWOOD OIL FACTORY

What a scent! This is where the sandalwood oil is extracted, in order to make perfume. They also sell soap, joss sticks, cosmetics and Ayurvedic products made of sandalwood, as well as sandalwood carvings. *Mon–Sat 9.30am–11am and 2pm–4pm | Manandavady Rd*

ENTERTAINMENT

HIGH OCTANE

The cool crowd parties at this fashionable club, with alternating themes directed by popular DJs and graphic light effects projected onto the walls. Admission for couples only. *2820 8th Cross Adipampa Rd, V.V. Mohalla | www. highoctanemys.com*

OPIUM

This pub in the Pai Vista Hotel is well-known for its loud heavy-rock music and the numerous portraits of rock stars decorating the walls. *Bangalore-Nilgiri Rd*

WHERE TO STAY

GREEN HOTEL ✪

This hotel has a total of 31 rooms, all with balcony and stylish wooden furniture. The best rooms are in the former Princess Palace, the cheaper ones in the new annexe. Standing in extensive grounds, it is run on environmentally friendly lines, with some of the profits going to environmental projects. *Chittaranjan Palace | 2270 Vinoba Rd, Jayalakshmipuram | tel. 0821 4 25 50 00 | www.greenhotelindia.com | Moderate*

LALITHA MAHAL PALACE

This former palace, which the vegetarian maharaja had built specially for his meat-eating guests, has often been used as a film set. The four-poster beds and antique furniture in each of the 54 rooms and suites convey a right-royal feeling. *Siddarth Nagar | tel. 0821 247 04 44 | www.lalithamahalpalace.in | Expensive*

RITZ HOTEL

It doesn't quite live up to its name – this establishment is a simple budget hotel near the zoo. It's been on the go for 60 years, has only ten rooms and a shady courtyard. *No. 12, Regency Theatre Complex, Lokaranjan Mahal Rd | tel. 0821 2 42 26 68 | www.hotelritzmysore.com | Budget*

INFORMATION

TOURIST RECEPTION CENTRE
Old Exhibition Building | Irwin Rd | tel. 0821 2 42 20 96

WHERE TO GO

NAGARHOLE NATIONAL PARK ★
(147 F5) (*𝄐 D9*)

Some 80 km/50 mi south of Mysore lies the Nagarhole National Park, the former hunting grounds of the Maharajas of Mysore. Today, monkeys do their acrobatics in trees and the park provides a habitat for more than 200 elephants, 100 tigers and over 50 leopards. There's lots for visitors to do in the park: jeep safaris, boat trips on the River Kabini, kayak and pedal boat tours, elephant rides and hikes. A lovely place to stay is the *Kabini River Lodge (Karapura, Nissana Beltur Post | tel. 08228 26 44 05 | www.kabiniriverlodge.com* or through *Jungle Lodges & Resorts Ltd. | Bengaluru | tel. 080 40 55 40 55 | www.junglelodges.com | Expensive)* with its 14 colonial-style double rooms, ten twin-bedded cottages in wooded surroundings and six tented cottages.

SRIRANGAPATNA (148 A5) (*𝄐 D9*)

This 5-km/3.1-mi long and 1-km/0.6-mi wide island lies 14 km/8.7 mi northeast of Mysore, surrounded by the Cauvery River (access via bridge). The sights of this former capital of the Wodeyar kings and stronghold of Tipu Sultan, the legendary 'Tiger of Mysore', can best be explored by bicycle. The *Old Fortress (daily 9am–5pm | free admission)* includes Captain Bailey's Dungeon, where British soldiers were held captive by Tipu Sultan. Within the fortress stands the *Sri Ranganathaswamy Temple (daily 7.30am–1pm and 4pm–9pm)* with its five-storey entrance gateway. The *Daria Daulat Bagh (Sat–Thu 9am–5pm | 200 Rs, video 25 Rs, only allowed in the garden)*, the 18th-century, two-storey summer palace of Tipu Sultan, was made entirely of teak and is notable for its murals and carved pillars. The *Gumbaz Mausoleum (Sat–Thu 8am–6pm | free admission)* with its white dome is the resting place of the sultan's family.

Peaceful times in Nagarhole National Park, the former hunting ground of the maharajas

AYURVEDA

★ *Ayurveda* is the knowledge of life. *Ayur* means science, *veda* means life. The ancient art of healing has its origins in India and has been passed down by word of mouth since around 600 BC. According to its doctrine, illnesses are caused by an imbalance in the three *doshas* (bioenergies), *vata, pitta* and *kapha. Vata* (space and air) controls all movement, *pitta* (fire and some water) the metabolism, and *kapha* (earth and water) takes care of structure and stability. During the initial examination, the Ayurveda doctor will determine by various diagnostic techniques, which *doshas* have fallen out of balance and by how much. This will be followed by customised treatments and diets.

Sometimes the methods take a little getting used to, such as the 'steam bath', where only your head protrudes from a wooden box. Or the 'Kerala massage' with the therapist using his or her feet, holding on to a rope for balance. The four-handed synchronised massage, *abhyangam*, is held to be extremely relaxing, as is *shirodhara* the stress-reducing oil poured on the forehead. Authentic Ayurveda does not allow the consumption of fish or meat during the course of treatment; bathing is also taboo. The patient therefore has to be very self-disciplined on that paradise beach. To this end, meditation and yoga help promote harmony between body, spirit and soul. Ayurveda is claimed to work particularly well during the ● monsoon, because the pores in the skin are wide open enabling more effective treatment. A two-week cleansing cure including accommodation and food in an Ayurveda resort will cost somewhere between 985 £/ 1255 US$ and 1500 £/1900 US$. An Ayurveda clinic is slightly cheaper.

AYURVEDA RESORTS

Most hotels in Kerala offer Ayurvedic massages. Ayurveda centres are certified by an *Olive Leaf* and officially accredited by the government in Kerala. A *Green Leaf* is awarded if the centre is also located in natural surroundings. Both accreditations are valid for three years. The directory can be found on the *Kerala Tourism* website, *www.keralatourism.org,* and it is also available through the *India Tourist Office (www.incredibleindia.com).* Reputable Ayurvedic resorts include: the

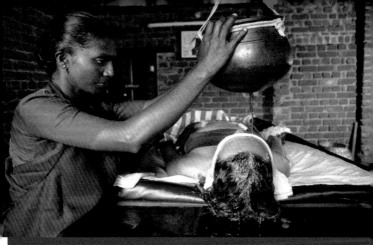

This ancient art of healing still works its magic – for both minor complaints and chronic conditions

cgh earth hotel *Kalari Kovilakom (tel. 04923 26 37 37 | www.kalarikovilakom. com)* housed in a former maharaja's palace; the *Thapovan Ayurvedic Centre* in Kovalam *(tel. 0471 2 48 04 53 | www. thapovan.com), the Somatheeram Ayurvedic Health Resort*, Kovalam, *(tel. 0471 2 26 81 01 | www.somatheeram. org)*, which has received numerous awards. The *Swaswara* (see p. 59) in Gokarna is heavily influenced by Ayurveda and yoga. The *Poovar Island Resort (tel. 0471 2 57 36 49 | www.poovarislandresort.com)* is situated on its own small island. Small, exclusive and stylish – that's the impression given by the ⊗ INSIDER TIP *Erandia Marari Ayurveda Beach Resort (tel. 0477 2 24 97 00 | www.erandiamarari. com)* with 6 bungalows and an infinity pool. Very rural and authentic is the ⊗ INSIDER TIP *Rajah Healthy Acres (tel. 0466 2 37 17 41)* located on 198 acres filled with healing plants in the hills of Thrissur.

AYURVEDA CLINICS

In Ayurveda resorts, the emphasis is mostly on treatments for internal body cleansing. In cases of chronic conditions such as rheumatism, diabetes, allergies, and cardiovascular or neurologically or metabolically related ailments, the best option is to go to a specialist Ayurvedic clinic such as the *Vaidya Ratnam Ayurveda Hospital* in Ollur/Thrissur *(tel. 0483 2 43 27 00 | www.vaidyaratnammooss.com)* or *AyurVaid (ayurvaid.com)*, India's first Ayurveda clinic to be certified according to international NABH clinical standards, which operates in Bangalore and Kochi. You can consult the competent portal *AyurvedaService* prior to your trip to check out the treatment offerings. Information: *www.ayurvedaservice.info/en*

KERALA

The 600-km/375-mi long Malabar Coast of southwest India corresponds exactly to the clichéd image of tropical beaches: warm as a bath, the Arabian Sea lapping against the endless stretches of palm-lined golden sand, beaches like Varkala with its red rocks, Alappuzha or the 9-km/5.5-mi long Kovalam Beach.

In the state of Kerala, which covers an area of 15,005 mi², you will find within a short distance the most diverse landscapes and climatic zones right next to each other: coconut palm forests (Kerala is named after the palm tree, *kera*), rice paddies, more than 40 rivers, hill stations in cool highlands with their tea, coffee, spice and rubber plantations, mountain tribes still living by the same rituals and according to the same rhythm they

have always done, powerful waterfalls thundering into the valleys and networks of trails stretching across hills and mountains. In between there are colonial cities and the enchanted world of the Backwaters, rainforests and jungle-like game reserves. A total of twelve nature reserves and two national parks provide protection for rare flora and fauna including the *Neelakurunji,* the blue flower, which blossoms only once every twelve years. Around 60 tigers live in the Periyar Tiger Sanctuary, while the Eravikulam National Park is home to the exotic Atlas moth and half the population of *Nilgiri tahr* – an endemic species of brown goat. Some of the world's rarest bird species can be found in the Thattekkady Bird Sanctuary; the Silent Valley National Park has a rel-

In the land where the peppercorn grows you're very close to paradise: India's loveliest holiday region is every traveller's dream

atively undisturbed evolutionary history stretching back at least 50 million years. And the Parambikulam Wildlife Sanctuary is one of the best places in the country to spot Indian bison, elephants and tigers. 'God's own country', as ex-Beatle Sir Paul McCartney calls Kerala, is fringed by glorious beaches, with everything from extensive luxury resorts to intimate boutique hotels to ecologically planned Ayurveda centres.

Indeed, ★ *Ayurveda* (see p. 64), the ancient Indian art of healing, runs like a thread through Kerala. No wonder, for this was where it all started thousands of years ago. Kerala sees itself as one big temple of wellness. All kinds of massages are offered at every corner, on every beach, in every small hotel, sometimes very professional, sometimes less so, but always extremely relaxing.

The land where the peppercorn grows is bordered by the Arabian Sea in the west and the Western Ghats, which in the hinterland rise to 2700 m/8850 ft. In 1502, the Portuguese mariner Vasco da Gama

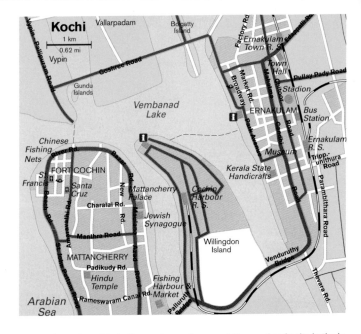

came ashore along this fertile coast on his third visit to India, with 15 ships and 800 men. But the booming trade in spices began over 2000 years ago and in the course of time it attracted Phoenicians, Greeks, Romans, Jews, Arabs, Chinese, Portuguese, Dutch and British. They all came back with an abundance of pepper, cardamom, sandalwood, cinnamon, ginger, saffron, tea, coffee and rubber.

In 1956, the rulers of the kingdoms of Malabar, Travancore and Cochin joined together to form the state of Kerala. Today, many different ethnic groups and religions live in peace with one another. Christianity got a foothold in Kerala earlier than elsewhere. In AD 52, 'Doubting Thomas', one of Jesus' Twelve Apostles, is said to have landed on the Malabar Coast. Kerala's educational attainment is higher than all the other Indian states. More than 90 percent of the approx. 32 mil-

lion population read and write in the local Malayalam language. This is thanks to the Maharani of Trivandrum, who in 1817 decided that the state would take over the entire cost of educating its citizens. In every town and village there is an elementary school within a radius of 3 km/1.9 mi. In the state of Kerala the government is alternately run by the CPI or the CPI (M), Communist Party of India (Marxist), and the Congress Party: in many places you'll see the Red Flag with hammer and sickle flying.

In recent years Kerala has been at the forefront of Indian efforts to solve ubiquitous environmental problems. Ecotourism is the buzzword, and the evidence that this has indeed been implemented in many hotel complexes is visible, tangible and palpable. The 600-km/375-mi coastline, stretching along the entire length of Kerala, is blessed with peaceful and often completely unspoilt, secluded sandy beaches. Offset by old lighthouses, nostalgic piers, high cliffs, fishing villages and impressive forts, each beach has its own character and charm. Nature and culture are the main aspects of a trip to Kerala. Kathakali, a sophisticated dance drama, casts every audience under its spell. Kerala also has a rich repertoire of classic martial arts, which can be traced back more than a thousand years. The festivals are much more than mere entertainment, being deeply rooted in the ancient traditions of Kerala.

KOCHI (COCHIN)

MAP ON PAGE 68
(150 A4) (*ₘ D11*)
Kerala' second-largest city (pop. 604,000) is considered the oldest European settlement in India.

On account of its picturesque situation in a natural harbour on the Malabar Coast and with its various districts that are spread across several peninsulas and outlying islands, Kochi is also called the 'Queen of the Arabian Sea'. On the mainland lies the district of Ernakulam. Ferries and bridges connect the islands of Willingdon, Bolghatty and Gundy in the harbour, Fort Cochin (which has retained the colonial name), Mattancherry at the southern end of the peninsula and Vallapadan and Vypeen north of Fort Cochin. Portuguese, Dutch and English settlers built most of the buildings in Fort Cochin, which is also the name given to the peninsula.

In the early morning, just off the beach at Fort Cochin, Kochi's particular brand of magic reveals itself to the visitor with the emergence of Chinese fishing nets being pulled out of the water with their abundant catch. Or in the evening, watching from a boat when the weird contraptions supporting the nets are etched as black

---

MARCO POLO HIGHLIGHTS

★ **Ayurveda**
Ancient knowledge: the fount of good health and long life originated in Kerala → p. 64, 67

★ **Chinese fishing nets**
These bizarre contraptions off the beach at Fort Cochin look like giant spiders → p. 70

★ **Kathakali**
Drums beat the rhythm in this classical dance drama → p. 73

★ **Brunton Boatyard**
A great view of the harbour from the former boatyard → p. 74

★ **Backwaters**
A vast network of enchanted waterways → p. 75, 92

★ **Marari Beach**
Picture postcard beach with palm trees → p. 76

★ **Munnar**
Living like a sahib among lush green tea plantations → p. 77

★ **Periyar Wildlife Sanctuary**
In South India's best-known nature reserve you can spot wild tigers, elephants and monkeys → p. 78

★ **Varkala**
Take tea here: money can't buy the sunset view from the cliff top → p. 88

★ **Kollam**
Fantastic location between lake and sea → p. 90

KOCHI (COCHIN)

(known as lift nets) are hopefully full to bursting, they are pulled up again. You can go along and buy ● freshly caught shrimps and have them cooked for you on the spot. If you arrive early in the morning the fishermen may actually invite you onto the jetties to watch the nets being raised. Merchants first introduced the Chinese fishing nets to Kerala in the 13th century. The nets make an impressive photo, particularly at sunset, and the view from ⚜ Vasco da Gama Square is one of the best. *Brunton Boatyard Hotel* has its own boat so that guests can see the sunset and the nets from the water. *Fort Cochin*

silhouettes against the setting sun. But Kochi's appeal also lies in the narrow alleyways of the Old Town with their many warehouses still wafting out their intense fragrance of spices. Kochi's history as a trading centre lives on in its grand colonial style mansions, in its old churches and in its continued importance as a busy fishing port.

SIGHTSEEING

BOLGHATTY PALACE
Built by the Dutch on Bolghatty Island in 1744, the former *Dutch Palace* was taken over by the British as their residence in 1909. Today it houses the *Hotel Bolghatty Palace*, which retains lots of the old colonial charm. Taking tea on the colonnaded veranda is a memorable experience. *Bolghatty Island | www.ktdc.com*

CHINESE FISHING NETS ★
Next to the ferry pier the beach is dominated by the distinctive Chinese fishing nets that are lowered into the water from a long cantilever supported by a bamboo frame anchored to a jetty. When the nets

DUTCH CEMETERY
This was laid out by the Dutch in 1724 and renovated in 2007. A visit to the cemetery is particularly worthwhile because of its special atmosphere with the 104 gravestones bearing the names of mainly Dutch, but also of British sailors, merchants and soldiers. Visits can be arranged with the nearby St Francis Church. *Right next to the beach at Fort Cochin*

INDO-PORTUGUESE MUSEUM
This museum is housed in the present-day Bishop's Residence, which was first built in 1506 for the Portuguese Governor. Its five sections are devoted to Kerala's Christian heritage and display a variety of artefacts including a beautifully carved teak altar dating from the 16th century and a sparkling crystal cross which refracts the sun's rays. *Tue–Sun 9am–1pm and 2pm–6pm | 25 Rs, first Thursday in the month admission free | Bishop House, Fort Cochin*

JEWISH QUARTER IN MATTANCHERRY
Narrow alleyways full of souvenir and antique shops: all the jewellery, furni-

ture and masks may look very tempting, but watch out for those export restrictions. It still gets very busy in the INSIDERTIP Spice Warehouses, also known as the *Spice Market*. Loads are hoisted to the lofts from brightly painted trucks. In the backyards are the large storerooms where you can buy spices very cheaply. The fragrance of nutmeg, cardamom, vanilla, cinnamon, sandalwood, ginger, coffee and tea wafts through the streets.

The *Paradesi Synagogue* is directly adjacent to the Mattancherry Palace. Built in 1568 by Jews whose forefathers arrived in Kerala as long ago as 69 BC, it is the oldest synagogue in India. As the last remaining of the seven synagogues that once stood in Cochin, it is used by the remaining Jewish community of about 20 souls. The floor of the synagogue is laid with blue and white Dutch tiles, and coloured-glass chandeliers hang from the ceiling. *Sun–Thu 10am–1pm and 3pm–5pm | access only barefoot | Synagogue Rd, Mattancherry*

SANTA CRUZ CATHEDRAL
At the southwestern tip of Fort Cochin and on the site of Kochi's first church built in 1505, stands the Roman Catholic cathedral. Constructed in 1903, it was modelled on the Rococo style and was only declared a cathedral in 1984, by Pope John Paul II. *Tue–Sat 9am–1pm and 2.30pm–4pm, Sun 10.30am–1pm, mass daily 6am, 7am and 6pm | 100 Rs | Rampath Rd, Fort Cochin | www.santacruzcathedralbasilica.org*

KERALA FOLKLORE THEATRE & MUSEUM
Today Kerala's folk art and artistic heritage are preserved in a former warehouse. The different architecture from three regions is displayed here: Malabar,

Cochin and Travancore. You can also see masks, dance costumes, musical instruments, dolls, sculptures and manuscripts inscribed on palm leaves. Certified antiques are sold in the museum shop. There are also theatre performances at random times (500 Rs). *Daily 9.30am–*

Magnificent colonial mix: the Paradesi Synagogue

7pm | 200 Rs, camera/video 100 Rs | Folklore Junction, Theavara, Kochi | tel. 0484 2 66 54 52

MATTANCHERRY PALACE/ DUTCH PALACE
This palace was built by the Portuguese in Mattancherry on the Fort Cochin peninsula in 1557 as a gift to the ruler of

Typical Kerala: red tile roofs around a courtyard characterise the Mattancherry Palace

the day, Raja Vira Keralavarma. It was restored by the Dutch in the mid-17th century and is hence also known as the Dutch Palace. The building is a typical example of traditional Keralan architecture: white exterior walls with red roof tiles and an interior courtyard. In the courtyard stands a small temple, but the best thing about this maharaja's palace is the collection of murals depicting scenes from the Hindu epic, the Ramayana. The maharaja's bedroom, with its own erotic murals, is not always open to the public. *Sat–Thu 10am–5pm | 5 Rs | Mattancherry*

ST FRANCIS CHURCH

Built by Franciscan monks, first of wood and in 1516 of stone, this is the oldest European church in India. The white facade with its curvy outline is typical of many churches in South India. Inside the building you will find the slab marking the original grave of Vasco da Gama, who died in Cochin around Christmas 1524.

His remains were later removed to Portugal. Other grave slabs bear the names of Portuguese and Dutch mariners. If the custodian is around, you might also get to see the old church books. *Mon–Sat 10am–5pm | Church Rd, Fort Cochin*

FOOD & DRINK

CAFÉ JEW TOWN

In the open *Ethnic Passage*, Annelies Damschen serves cappuccino, fresh juices, chocolate and cheesecake as well as other European specialities. *The Ethnic Passage, Mattancherry, Fort Cochin | tel. 0484 6 06 87 16 | Moderate*

INSIDER TIP CAFÉ PORT VIEW ☼

With its views over the red rooftops of the Old Town and a pleasant cooling breeze, the roof terrace of the New Castle Gallery is an ideal place for a break. There's an old telescope on hand to enhance the amazing views that extend as far as Willingdon Island. The café serves Indian snacks, sandwiches and curries. *Bazaar Rd, Mattancherry | tel. 0484 2 2107 37 | Budget*

KASHI
This is an interesting mixture of art gallery and restaurant. You can get Italian cappuccino and *chai masala* – Indian spiced tea. There's also a small selection of European dishes on the breakfast and lunch menus. *Burgher St, Fort Cochin | tel. 0484 2 2157 69 | www.kashiartgallery. com | Budget–Moderate*

SEAGULL
Here you'll find good quality at very reasonable prices. Relax on the terrace while looking out over the harbour. Buffet at lunchtime. *2–18 Calvathy Rd, Fort Cochin | tel. 0484 2 21 81 28 | Budget*

SHOPPING

In Ernakulam, *Mahatma Gandhi Road*, otherwise known as MG Road, and *Broadway* are the main shopping thoroughfares. From Oriental and Western clothing to jewellery, cheap bags and suitcases, you can find (almost) everything here.

THE ETHNIC PASSAGE
This trendy arcade lies at the heart of the Mattancherry's Jewish quarter and houses bookstores, art galleries, leather shops and antique stores. *Mattancherry, Fort Cochin*

FABINDIA
Traditional patterns and fabrics produced in chic designs; there are several branches in Kochi: *Edapally, Bldg. 34/138 L2, 1st*

KATHAKALI

★ ● *Kathakali* is dance drama and the best-known dance form in South India. Silently, but with strong facial expressions and gestures, dancers enact scenes from the Hindu epics Ramayana and Mahabharata. The various characters are distinguished by the different colours of make-up on their faces. The long make-up process is seen as part of the whole performance, and spectators are very welcome to watch. The oldest and best Kathakali demonstration is offered by the *See India Foundation*. The make-up ceremony can be seen at 6pm and the daily performances begin at 6.45pm. *Admission 300 Rs | Kalathi Parambil Lane 7, Ernakulam | tel. 0484 2 37 64 71*

The *Kerala Kathakali* Centre also stages the dance drama with an explanation of the gestures and colours before the show begins, daily 6.30pm (make-up procedure at 5pm). They also have daily performances of classical Indian music, and other Kerala dances on Saturdays (8.45pm). *Admission 300 Rs | K. B. Jacob Rd, Fort Cochin | tel. 0484 2 2158 27 | www.kathakalicentre.com*
In *Greenix Village*, as well as traditional dances and martial arts they also demonstrate *Mohiniyattam* – a soft, flowing dance style with round movements, modelled on those of temple dancers. Make-up starts at 5pm, the dances at 6pm. *Admission 300 Rs | Kalvathy Rd, Fort Cochin | tel. 0484 2 2170 00 | www.greenix.in*

floor, opposite Eastern Edapally; Lulu Mall Edapally, Shop No. F10, 1st floor, Lulu International Shopping Mall; Oberon Mall, Shop 9, 1st floor, Bypass – Edapally | www.fabindia.com

THE KERALA STATE HANDICRAFTS DEVELOPMENT CORPORATION SHOWROOM – KAIRALI

Long name, big choice and fixed prices in this state-run emporium for handicrafts, materials, jewellery and much more. *MG Rd (at Jose Junction), Ernakulam | www.keralahandicrafts.in*

INSIDER TIP LITTLE QUEEN EMBROIDERY ⚫

Even Prince Charles and Duchess Camilla looked at the reasonably priced bobbin lace and petit-point embroidery – the smallest in the world with 3200 stitches per inch/ca. 2.5 cm – in the small but beautiful shop. The handicrafts are produced by 286 fishermen's wives and widows. *Synagogue Lane, IV/542, Jewish Quarter, Mattancherry*

INSIDER TIP NEW CASTLE GALLERY

Three floors packed full of art, jewellery, carpets, perfume, pashmina shawls. Bargaining essential. Purchases are also shipped. *Bazaar Rd, Mattancherry*

ENTERTAINMENT

AVA LOUNGE

Kochi's chic nightspot is in the *Dream Cochin* boutique hotel. Named after the film star Ava Gardner, the style is completely femme fatale: burnished golden sofas, gorgeous cushions, pure glamour. The mix of disco and nightclub attracts mainly Kochi's young smart set – not least on account of the steep (for India) admission price. *Closed Sun | admission 2500 Rs, Wed usually ladies night (free admission for women) | S. A. Rd, Kadavanthara | www.dreamcochin.com*

EVENING BOAT TRIP

A romantic boat tour at sunset, once the temperatures have cooled – just delightful! With views of the harbour, Marine Drive, Bolgatty Island, Willingdon Island and the fishing nets. The tours depart from the harbour. *Daily 5.30pm–7pm | booking through the Tourism Reception Centre KTDC | Shanmugham Rd | tel. 0484 2 35 32 34 | www.ktdc.com*

WHERE TO STAY

BRUNTON BOATYARD ★

This hotel occupies a beautifully restored Victorian shipyard right on the harbour. The 22-room luxury establishment has an outdoor pool overlooking the water and the open arcades surrounding the shady inner courtyard are furnished with antiques. *River Rd, Fort Cochin | tel. 0484 2 21 54 61 | wwrw.cghearth.com | Expensive*

CHITTOOR KOTTARAM

Something completely different: live like a king! Only closed groups of max. six people can stay at the 200-year-old residence of Keralan King Raja Verma, located on a backwater channel (1 large and 2 small bedrooms). Guests enjoy exclusive privacy, but convention dictates that they go barefoot inside. Service is top notch: the cooks prepare Keralan vegetarian specialities. *Chittoor Temple, opposite the SDOA School, Kottaram Rd, Vaduthala | tel. 0484 3 01 17 11 | www.cghearth.com/chittoor-kottaram | Expensive*

SPENCER HOME

The eleven rooms in this old Portuguese house are large and well maintained, and each one enjoys a view of the lovely garden. *1/298 Parade Rd, Fort Cochin | tel.*

0484 2 2150 49 | spencerhome-fortkochi. blogspot.com | Budget

SPICE FORT
This boutique hotel in the heart of Fort Cochin has 27 rooms and a pool in the courtyard. In the restaurant guests are

right on the Arabian Sea and fully lives up to the epithet bestowed on it by Viceroy Lord Curzon. The city (pop. 177,000) was laid out around two canals in the year 1776.

Alappuzha, with its endless palm groves, is also a good starting point for excursions

Backwaters supermarket: where merchants offer their wares from the water

served organic food; in the lounge, the hotel's organic coffee is served. *Princess St | tel. 0484 2 2189 81 | www.duneeco group.com | Moderate*

INFORMATION

TOURIST INFORMATION CENTRE
At the pier | Ernakulum | tel. 0484 2 35 03 00; River Rd, at the bus station, Kumalakadavu | Fort Cochin | tel. 0484 2 2165 67

WHERE TO GO

ALAPPUZHA (ALLEPPEY)
(150 A4) (*ω D12*)
This so-called 'Venice of the East' lies

along the ★ *Backwaters* (see p. 92), Kerala's tightly woven network of canals, lakes, lagoons and 44 rivers in total that is unique in the world. Many migratory birds spend the winter in this mostly untouched paradise.

In fact, most of the Backwater tours begin in Alappuzha. Some 900 km/560 mi of the 1900 km/1180 mi of waterways are navigable. Alappuzha is linked by waterway to Kollam in the south and to Kottayam in the east. There are regular ferry connections between the three cities. Especially picturesque is the palm-lined *Alappuzha Beach,* complete with its lighthouse and pier. The lighthouse is more than 170 years old and has often featured in Bollywood movies.

Kottayam District is also home to the small town of *Kumarakom*. Here, the former teacher Raji Punnoose runs the INSIDERTIP *Bay Island Driftwood Museum* (Tue–Sat 10am–5pm, Sun 11.30am–5pm | Chakranpadi | www.bayislandmuseum.com). There is nothing else like it in India: for 25 years she has gathered driftwood from the Andaman and Nicobar Islands and has created from it a quite extraordinary artistic collection. The best hotel in the area, the *Vivanta by Taj Kumarakom* (28 rooms | Kumarakom, Kottayam | tel. 0481 2525711 | www.vivantabytaj.com | Moderate–Expensive), lies on Vembanad Lake, a Backwater lagoon. The main building is the 125-year-old *Bakers Bungalow*. Small villas built in Keralan style are ranged around the large pool and are partly furnished with antiques. The INSIDERTIP *Coconut Palms Resort* (Thottapally, Kumarakodi, Pallana, Alleppey | tel. 0471 3 01 81 00 | www.coconutpalms.co.in | Budget) has its own houseboat and a lot of charm. It is a 200-year-old Keralan-style house with columned veranda, sweeping roof and eight charming rooms, just 400 m/1312 ft from the Backwaters and 100 m/328 ft from the almost deserted *Pallana Beach*. Ayurveda, canoes and bicycles are also available. The INSIDERTIP *Harbour Beer & Wine Bar* (Beach Rd | tel. 0477 2 23 97 67 | www.raheemresidency.com | Expensive) next to the *Raheem Residency* boutique hotel, is a popular place to congregate, especially to watch the sun set over the ocean. For food, the *Kream-Korner Art Café* is recommended (Mullakal | tel. 0477 2 26 00 05 | kreamkornerartcafe.com | Budget), and displays contemporary art. A varied selection of *thali* is served here. Souvenir idea: some shops along the *Mullackal Shopping Street* sell brightly-painted umbrellas. *50 km/31.1 mi south*

CHERAI BEACH �► (150 A4) (*D11*)
Kill two birds with one stone: sunrise over the Backwaters, then sunset over the sea. Both are possible from the same place, the glorious beach at the northern end of Vypeen Island, lined by dense palm groves and green rice fields. *By ferry (30 min) from Ernakulum*

ELEPHANT CAMP (150 B4) (*D11*)
Situated 45 km/28 mi northeast of Kochi is the village of Kodanad, at the edge of the Periyar National Park. At the time of the maharajas it was considered the largest elephant camp in South India. Since the introduction of a ban on elephant capture in 1977, Kodanad has just been a training centre for elephants. It's fun to watch the baby elephants as they bathe in the Periyar river morning and evening. *Mon–Sat 8am–5pm, Sun 8am–noon | Abhayaranyam | Kaprikkad | tel. 0484 2 64 90 52*

HILL PALACE MUSEUM TRIPUNITHURA (150 A4) (*D11*)
This former residence of the king of Cochin has been converted into the largest ethno-archaeological museum in Kerala. The palace, built on a hill in 1865, comprises 49 separate buildings. Exhibits are arranged in 18 galleries and include amongst other items the royal throne, the crown, portraits of the ruler, 14th-century carvings, jewellery, porcelain and old musical instruments. *Tue–Sun 9am–5pm | 250 Rs | 10 km/6.2 mi southeast*

MARARI BEACH ★ (150 A5) (*D12*)
Located 70 km/43.5 mi south of Kochi is the most beautiful beach in Kerala – Marari Beach on the so-called 'Spice Coast'. Still largely undiscovered by mass tourism, this glorious idyll, with its fine sand, palm groves, small fishing villag-

es and palm huts, is the perfect place to unwind. The *Hotel Marari Beach (Mararikulam, Alappuzha | tel. 0484 3 01 17 11 | www.cghearth.com | Moderate)*, has 52 Kerala-style bungalows and blends harmoniously with the landscape, hammocks swaying between some of the 3000-odd palm trees in the ground. It also grows its own organic fruit and vegetables.

MUNNAR ⭐ (150 B4) (*𝄐 E11*)

On account of their highland vegetation, the *Kanan Devan Hills* are often referred to as the Scotland of India. Nestled in the Western Ghats at a height of 1600 m/5249 ft, between the Mudrapuzha, Nallathanni and Kundala rivers, lies the pretty mountain town of Munnar (pop. 68,000). In colonial times the British came here for the cooler climes. Rising nearby is the highest mountain in South India, the 2695-m/8842-ft Anamudi, but climbing to the summit is not allowed because of the delicate vegetation.

For mile after mile, rolling tea plantations stretch across the hillside, and 50 tons of tea are harvested in Munnar and its surrounding villages every single day. The *Tea Museum (daily 10am–4.30pm | 125 Rs)* explains how the tea is processed and shows a film about its history; you can also buy tea straight from the producers, at very reasonable prices. Visiting a tea plantation can be arranged through the *Tourist Office (Main Rd | tel. 04865 23 15 16)*. The public paths snaking through the hilly plantations are perfect for hiking. It's also well worth visiting the *Atukkad Falls,* 8 km/5 mi from Munnar, in the gorge at Pallivasal. A relative trickle for most of the year, during the monsoon in July and August it becomes a roaring cascade and home to sizeable colonies of birds. The route also leads past the ☆ *Pothamedu* viewpoint (6 km/3.7 mi from Munnar),

Lots of effort for one small cup: tea is still harvested by hand

which offers glorious views over the green waves of geometrically arranged tea gardens. About 7 km/4.4 mi from Munnar is *Devikulam,* an idyllic mountain village. The INSIDERTIP flower meadow on the shores of Sita Devi Lake is a wonderful picnic spot. A further hiking destination lies 10 km/6.2 mi away: *Yaymakad,* a beautiful area full of waterfalls, which plunge as much as 160 m/525 ft into the depths. It is to a coffee rather than a tea plantation that the hotel *Windermere Estate (Poathamedu, Munnar | tel. 0486 5 23 05 12 | www.windermeremunnar.com | Moderate–Expensive)* belongs. Here you will have a 360° panorama of the summits of the Western Ghats. A variety of exclusive garden villas with a total of 21 very tastefully furnished rooms blends harmoniously into the spectacular landscape. Accommodation of an unusual kind is provided at the INSIDERTIP *Munnar Rock Resort (2nd Mile, Pallivasal, Munnar | tel. 0828 1 99 72 92 | www.munnarrock. com | Moderate),* which is perched, like a tree house, on top of an enormous cliff. There are only two rooms at the summit, a further six at the foot of the cliff. *130 km/81 mi east*

PERIYAR WILDLIFE SANCTUARY ★
(150 B4) (*E12*)
At an elevation of between 900–1800 m/ 2953–5906 ft and easily reached by bus is the *Periyar Wildlife Sanctuary (daily 6am–6pm | admission 300 Rs),* which stretches across an area of 300 mi². It was declared a tiger reserve in 1978. If you take a boat excursion on Periyar Lake, something that can be organised in Thekkady, you'll be able to spot entire herds of bathing elephants. Bookings can be made through the *Tiger Reserve Organisation (Ambady Junction, Lake Rd, Thekkady | tel. 04869 22 45 71 | www. periyarfoundation.online)* or through

the *Forest Information and Reservation Centre (tel. 04869 32 20 28)* in the same building. There are many different activities available, such as hiking for 500 Rs, *Periyar Tiger Trail* (trekking and camping) for 6500 Rs, *Bamboo Rafting* for 2000 Rs per person. Further information: *Tourism Information Thekkady (Junction in Kumily | tel. 04869 22 26 20 or at www.peri yartiger reserve.org)*

If possible, try to stay the night in Thekkady. The 55 thatched cabins of the ⊕ INSIDERTIP *Spice Village (tel. 04869 22 45 14 | www.cghearth.com/spice-vil lage | Moderate–Expensive)* are laid out like a tribal mountain village, in lush grounds covering an area of about 15 acres. In a live show *(daily 7.30pm–9.30pm),* a ranger tells you all about the wild animals that lurk around the perimeter; at cooking classes you can learn the secrets of the local cuisine and how to use and combine spices. This establishment puts the *experience not luxury* at the forefront, so everything from trekking to boat tours in the Periyar National Park as well as visits to spice and peppercorn farms is on offer. In addition they have a pool and offer Ayurveda. Because of their exemplary use of natural resources (their own paper recycling, organic vegetables, no TV, no air conditioning) the lodge has received numerous awards since it opened.

The Wildernest (Thekkady Rd | tel. 04869 22 40 30 | www.wildernest-kerala.com | Budget–Moderate) is a good B & B option. It is designed using natural materials, has ten bright, attractive rooms, some with balcony, others a small garden. The hearty breakfast should set you up for the entire day. *185 km/115 mi southeast*

THRISSUR (TRICHUR)
(150 A3) (*D11*)
Due to its rich history and architectural treasures, 'the city of Lord Shiva' is re-

Elephants parading side by side during the Pooram Festival at the Vadakkunathan Temple

garded as the cultural capital of Kerala. For centuries Thrissur (pop. 318,000) belonged to the royal house of Kochi. Many rulers and dynasties, as well as colonial powers like Holland and Britain, were involved in the political and cultural growth of the city and its region. Splendid temples and remarkable churches bear witness to these developments.

Beautifully situated on a hill, surrounded by four *gopuram* (temple towers), the *Vadakkunnathan Temple (daily 4am–10am and 5pm–8pm)* dates from the 12th century. The walls of the temple are adorned with exquisite murals, the wooden beams decorated with beautiful carvings. In April/May, during the Pooram Festival, the temple is also the destination of the grand procession of ornately decorated elephants. However, non-Hindus are forbidden from entering the temple, though they can set foot in the yard and walk around the outer wall. The *Guruvayur Ksetram Temple*, 30 km/18.6 mi northwest of Thrissur, is one of the most famous in all Kerala. Alongside the

temple you can also visit the *Guruvayur Devaswom Institute (Mon–Fri 8am–4pm)* to see how the art of wall painting is taught. The towers of the Basilica of Our *Lady of Dolours,* also known as Puthan Palli ('new church'), soar over the city. From the 87-m/285.4-ft high ☀ *Bible Tower (Tue–Fri 10am–1pm and 2pm–7.30pm, Sat–Sun 10am–1pm and 2pm–7.30pm | High Rd)* you can enjoy a stunning panoramic view. The shining white building claims to be the largest church in Asia and is famous for its Indogothic style. Its foundation stone was laid in 1929, but the basilica was only consecrated in 1940. The Cathedral of Our *Lady of Lourdes* is best known for its underground chapel. *50 km/31.1 mi north*

KOZHIKODE (CALICUT)

(147 F6) (*D10*) **It is claimed that Vasco da Gama first stepped ashore on Indian**

soil at **Kappad Beach. At least that's what the memorial plaque that has been erected there says. The date was 20 May 1498.** Historians think, however, that he actually landed at nearby Panthalayini in Kollam. Even the Italian globetrotter Marco Polo praised the beauty of Calicut. Today the *Jewel of Malabar* (pop. 550,000) offers a mixture of old temples, mosques, churches, markets and shopping thoroughfares. At the heart of the city is *Mananchira Square,* once the

tre by the sea, comes alive with people strolling and inline skating.

SIGHTSEEING

MISHKAL MOSQUE

It was about 700 years ago that an Arab ship owner by the name of Nakhooda Mishkal had this mosque built. Constructed on 24 carved columns, it has a total of 47 doors and is primarily made of wood. Because the minaret is missing and the

A very welcoming place: the Mishkal Mosque has 47 doors

gigantic courtyard of a palace. Now the square is a green oasis with an artificial stream and an open-air stage for music and theatre. There are still a few colonial buildings standing in the old centre of the city, but many of the beautiful original houses have been replaced by modern functional structures – the city is gradually losing its character.

Kozhikode has a lot going on in the evening in particular. It is then that families set up their picnics on Mananchira Square, and the 3-km/1.9-mi long Beach Road, some 2 km/1.2 mi outside the cen-

entrance looks more like a *gopuram,* the mosque bears a strong resemblance to Kerala's temple architecture. *Kuttichari, 2 km/1.2 mi outside Kozhikode*

PAZHASSIRAJA MUSEUM

This bungalow that once belonged to the Kottayam royal family dates from 1812. On display inside are murals, antique bronzes, ancient coins and crockery, while the art gallery next door exhibits the collections of various members of the royal family. *Tue–Sun 9am–1pm and 2pm–4.30pm | 20 Rs | East Hill | Karaparambu*

ST MARY'S CSI CHURCH

Dating from 1842, the largest Basel Mission church of the Malabar region is also known as the *English Church*. *The Evangelical Missionary Society of Basel* was founded in Switzerland in 1815, and one of its most important areas of operations was South India. St Mary's CSI Church has the only pipe organ in Kerala, a gift from St Ayden's Church in Cheltenham, England. *Daily 10am–1pm | Kannur Rd*

FOOD & DRINK

DAKSHIN

This very reasonably priced, purely vegetarian establishment is the best place to go for *dosas,* pizza and simple rice dishes. *17/43 Mavoor Rd | tel. 0495 2 72 26 48 | Budget*

KINGSBAY

This bright, friendly restaurant specialises in fish and seafood. Young people and travellers in particular appreciate the relaxed atmosphere and the view through the large window. *1414 Customs Rd | tel. 075598 7 78 77 | Moderate*

THE PARAGON RESTAURANT

Seafood features prominently at this upscale restaurant in the heart of the city. The art of authentic Malabar cuisine has been celebrated here ever since 1939 with dishes such as *Malabar Biryani* and *Coconut Chili Shrimps.* To go with them they mix their own original mocktails. *Kannur Rd | tel. 0495 2 76 10 | www.paragonrestaurant.net | Moderate–Expensive*

SHOPPING

SM Street, actually *Sweet Meat Street,* is the main shopping thoroughfare in Kozhikode. Here they sell everything that the holidaymaker's heart desires – trendy clothes, modern jewellery and local handicrafts.

CAPITAL INTERNATIONAL BOOKS

You could browse in this bookshop for hours on end. The selection is diverse, and the prices for English-language books very low. You might even unearth a title here that you hadn't been able to find anywhere else. *1st floor, Mavoor Rd*

MALABAR BAKERY

This is where you'll find the very best black *Calicut halwa,* a sweet that originally comes from the Arab World and is considered a Kozhikode speciality. *Kallai Rd, opposite Pushpa Theatre, Tali*

NUTAN HANDICRAFTS

A good place for souvenirs such as hand-embroidered fabrics of silk and cotton, statues of deities and beautiful woven napkins and tablecloths. *YMCA Shopping Complex, Kannur Rd | www.nutanhandicrafts.com*

BEACHES IN THE VICINITY

BEKAL (147 E5) (*⑪ C9*)

Deserted beaches, palm trees, Bekal Fort – the best preserved fortress in Kerala – and very peaceful, new resorts: Bekal is the new holiday region in the far north of Kerala on the Malabar Coast, 16 km/9.9 mi south of Kasaragod and 192 km/119 mi north of Calicut. Its potential was only recently discovered and is now gradually being realised. The *Fort* (*daily 8am–6pm | admission 200 Rs*) was built in the 17th century and is located on a rocky promontory between two sandy beaches. An easily accessible ramp leads to the lookout tower. The ancient *Anjenaya Temple* with its idols in the stucco wall and an old mosque, said to have been built by Tipu Sultan, demonstrate the tolerance of different religions.

The smartest resort is *The Lalit (Padinhar Rd, Udma | tel. 04672 23 77 77 | www.thelalit.com | Expensive)* on the long beach to the north of the fort. Its Balinese-style buildings contain only 37 rooms spread across 26 acres of lush green. Each one is a flexible space and has its own private outdoor jacuzzi. Romantic dinners can be arranged on the anchored *Kettuvalam houseboat (8 rooms)*. There's almost too much service: a 'holiday host' is on hand for every room. The spa also offers a large range of treatments.

BEYPORE BEACH (147 F6) (*M D10*)

This glorious sandy beach lies some 10 km/6.2 mi south of Kozhikode. It is famous for its boatyard, where traditional *dhows* have been built ever since around 1500; today they still cast off from the beach in all directions.

KAPPAD BEACH (147 F6) (*M D10*)

It is on this palm-lined beach that Vasco da Gama is believed to have landed with his three ships on 20 May 1498. A temple thought to be more than 800 years old stands on the rocks. It has now been restored and painted in yellow, gold and black. Inside the building there is a platform *(peeda)*, which is worshipped as the seat of Bhadrakali, an incarnation of Goddess Parvati. Because she carries so many weapons with her, there are several golden swords with scimitar blades hanging in the temple. *16 km | 9.9 mi north*

KOZHIKODE BEACH (147 F6) (*M D10*)

This beach is famous for its sunsets. For a few rupees you can eat at one of the many stalls selling specialities such as *kallumekaya* (mussels). The old lighthouse and two piers, both over 100 years old, lend the beach a special charm.

PADINHAREKARA BEACH ✂️ (150 A3) (*M D11*)

At the end of Tipu Sultan Road in Ponnani, 50 km/31.1 mi south of Kozhikode,

Martial arts à la Kalari: where it takes years of training to jump over the small stick

this beach provides a good vantage point from which to view the estuary of the Bharathapuzha River as it flows into the Arabian Sea.

INSIDER TIP **VALLIKUNNU BEACH**

(147 F6) (*D10*)

This paradise beach lies 27 km/16.8 mi south of Kozhikode and is completely lined with palm trees. From here the *Kadalundi Bird Sanctuary* can be reached on foot.

ENTERTAINMENT

CVN KALARI SANGAM

This is where you can see Kerala's very own martial art. Adversaries skilfully dodge each other as they lunge with swords and sticks, in a combat that depends on alertness and agility, using various steps and swift movements. *Daily 5pm–7pm | 250 Rs per performance | Nadakkavu | tel. 0495 2 76 82 91 | www.cvnkalari.com*

WHERE TO STAY

ALAKAPURI GUEST HOUSE

Established in 1958, this hotel stands in a delightful garden with a lotus pond and an abundance of flowers and trees. Its 40 spacious rooms have comfortable, old-style furniture, and there is a good restaurant and bar. The hotel is definitely one of the best in its category. *Moulana Mohamed Ali Rd, near the station | tel. 0495 27 23 45 | Budget*

INSIDER TIP **NEELESHWAR HERMITAGE** ✹

This epitome of a tropical paradise lies rather hidden among the palm trees on a secluded beach, where hammocks swing between the trees, pheasants strut around, tortoises are reared and an infinity pool seems to drop straight into the ocean. With no fewer than 18 thatched cottages all furnished in natural materials, the *Priya Spa* offers wellness, Ayurveda and yoga, plus the chef gives cooking classes. *Ozhinhavalappu, Kasaragod | tel. 0467 2 28 75 10 | www.neeleshwar hermitage.com | Moderate–Expensive*

OYSTER OPERA RESORT

Named after its owner – an oyster farmer who still uses traditional methods – this unusual resort is beautifully located on a promontory. The seven simple bamboo cottages, stilt and tree houses have names like 'Mussel', 'Oyster' and 'Shrimp'. The resort's own houseboat cruises through the backwaters. The resort was cleaned up and plastic bottles were removed. *Tel. 0467 2 27 81 01 | www.oysteropera.in | Budget*

RAVIZ KADAVU RESORT ✹

As an Ayurveda resort, this establishment has been awarded Kerala's Green Leaf certification. The typical Kerala-style building has been here ever since the 11th century and is situated in a beautiful tropical garden right on the Backwaters. There are 97 rooms, 6 suites and 17 cottages and from the balconies and terraces, as well as one of the two restaurants (the *open-air Makkani* by the pool), you can watch the shimmering green Chaliyar River. A doctor monitors the Ayurveda treatments, which are applied very seriously. In addition, yoga and cookery courses as well as houseboat tours are offered. *Calicut Bypass Rd, Azhinjilam | tel. 0495 2 41 11 11 | www.theraviz.com | Expensive*

RENAI KAPPAD BEACH RESORT

This charming complex is located in a palm grove on the beach, with a pool. All of the four cottages have four rooms, each one enjoying a view of the ocean. It's the perfect place for an Ayurvedic cure. *Thoovappara Kappad | tel. 0496 2 68 87 77 | kappadbeachresort.in | Moderate–Expensive*

INFORMATION

TOURIST INFORMATION DTPC
Very helpful. *Manachira | tel. 0495 2 72 00 12*

TOURIST OFFICE
Kozhikode Railway Station | tel. 0495 2 70 23 04

WHERE TO GO

KANNUR (147 E5) (*ⅅ C9*)
Here, the old fort and the Parassinika-davu Temple are well worth a visit. In 1505 the first Portuguese viceroy, Dom Francesco de Almeida, had the *St Angelo Fort (daily 8am–6pm | admission free)* strategically built on a rocky outcrop. Even today, visitors can see the dungeons, the secret passages leading to the sea, an old chapel and some cannons. Situated 18 km/11.2 mi to the northeast, the *Parassinikadavu Sri Muthappan Temple (daily 5am–8am and 4pm–8pm)* stands on the banks of the Valapattnam River, a popular place of pilgrimage. Legend has it that a child worked a miracle here. The holy shrine is even open to visitors. Information: *Tourist Office | Thaluk Office Compound | tel. 0497 2 70 63 36. 90 km/55.9 mi north*

 **MAHÉ** (147 F6) (*ⅅ C10*)
Also known as Mayyazhi, this charming little town (pop. 45,000) is situated on the estuary of the Mahé River. Its distinctly French atmosphere dates back to the time when it was an important French trading enclave. The police here continue to wear red caps just like in France, streets have French names and many of the locals speak the language of the early merchants. Its lovely riverside promenade is lined by old lanterns. *St Theresa's Church* is one of the oldest churches in the Malabar region, built in 1736 by the Italian Father Dominic. *65 km/40.4 mi north*

 WAYANAD (147 F5–6) (*ⅅ D10*)
In the Nilgiri Hills, 105 km/65 mi northeast of Kozhikode, the region of Wayanad, including the national park of the same name (133 mi²) *(admission 300 Rs)*, is only just being discovered. But the tourist invasion hasn't arrived yet. Only a few nature lovers come here, to see the caves, go trekking in the jungle and marvel at the variety of exotic wildlife. Or get to know the *Adivasi* – the indigenous hill folk – and join them in celebrating the monsoon at the ● *Monsoon Splash festival* in Kalpetta – complete with mud football, crab racing, ox-cart or raft rides. Further information: *Wayanad Tourism Organisation | Civil Station, Kalpetta | tel. 04936 20 21 34 | www. wayanadtourism.org*

THIRUVA-NANTHAPU-RAM (TRIVAN-DRUM)

MAP INSIDE BACK COVER
(150 B6) (*ⅅ E13*) **Magnificent colonial buildings characterise Kerala's capital city of Thiruvananthapuram with its 785,000 inhabitants.**

Just like Rome, the 'City of Sacred Snakes'' was built on seven hills. Red roof tiles, modern shops and small cafés

WHERE TO START?
East Fort/Museum Square:
you can reach East Fort with buses 581 and 609 (orange), and nos. 5 and 8 will take you to Museum Square. Linking these two points is *Mahatma Ghandi Road*. From East Fort to the west of the station it's a short walk to the Sri Padmanabha Swamy Temple and to the Chalai Bazaar. On Museum Square you'll find, for example, the Napier and Kerala Museums, as well as various galleries. The zoo is also nearby.

SIGHTSEEING

KUTHIRAMALIKA PALACE

This enormous two-storey palace with more than 80 rooms is also known as the *Puthen Mailika*. It was built in 1844 for Maharaja Swathi Thirunal, in typical Keralan style, with magnificent carvings and life-size figures. Some parts of the building have been turned into a museum. Outstanding carved exhibits include the 140-year-old ivory throne and wooden horses in the upper gallery, as well as palanquins, weapons and life-size Kathakali mannequins. *Tue–Sun 8.30am–1pm and 3pm–5.30pm | 50 Rs | East Fort*

reinforce the European impression. In addition, the former Trivandrum is important as the setting-off point for Kerala's most popular beach, Kovalam. It lies just 16 km/9.9 mi to the south and can easily be reached by bus or motor-rickshaw.

NAPIER MUSEUM

Also known as the *Thiruvananthapuram Museum*. Designed in 19th-century red-and-white Indo-Sarenic style, the building is impressive enough on its own. But it also houses a large collection of South Indian art, including statues of bronze

A real challenge for all the senses: the daily bustle of Trivandrum's streets

and wood from the 11th–18th century, jewellery from the 10th–14th century, a temple chariot of rosewood with carved mythological figures from 1847 and a replica of a typical Keralan house. *Daily 10am–4.45pm | 25 Rs | Public Park*

Every morning, at varying times according to the season, hundreds of Hindus congregate in the courtyard of this black stone temple to smash between 20,000 and 30,000 coconuts as an offering to the elephant-headed god Ganesh. A loud murmur like a swarm of bees echoes around the courtyard for while breaking the coconuts the faithful offer a prayer. The local statue of *Lord Ganapathy* (Ganesh) is so strongly revered here because, unusually, the right leg of the god is bent as if in the lotus posture. *East Fort*

SRI CHITRA ART GALLERY
This gallery is situated opposite the Napier Museum and amongst other items displays pictures by the painter Raja Rai Varma (1848–1906), known for his detailed depictions of scenes from the religious epics Mahabharata and Ramayana. In addition, there are exquisite works by Rajputs and Moghuls, who at various times had a huge influence on the cultural development of India. *Tue, Thu–Sun 10am–4.45pm, Mon and Wed before noon only | 25 Rs | Public Park*

SRI PADMANABHA SWAMY TEMPLE
In June 2011 this temple achieved overnight fame, because in two of its six underground chambers, which had been closed for 130 years, a hoard of treasure worth approx. 7–9 billion £/8–11 billion US$ was discovered, amassed from the donations of former benefactors in the form of diamonds, rubies, emeralds, gold and silver. Dating from the 17th century, the temple is dedicated to the god Vishnu. Its 17-m/55.8-ft high entrance tower is visible from afar. Non-Hindus can only admire the holy temple from the outside, but twice a year everyone has a chance to glimpse the gilded statue of Sri Padmanabha, an incarnation of Vishnu: in March/April and in October/November, when it is carried to the sea for a ritual bath. *At the southern end of the MG Rd*

ZOO
The large park was opened by the Maharaja of Travancore in 1859 as one of the first zoological gardens in India. Laid out like a botanic garden, with its many trees, lakes and lawns it is considered the most natural zoo in the country. It is home to a total of 75 animal species, including such rare specimens as the Bengal tiger and the Asian lion. *Tue–Sun 9am–6.15pm | 25 Rs, camera 10 Rs, video camera 100 Rs | PMG Junction*

FOOD & DRINK

INSIDER TIP ▶ ARYA NIVAS

The best vegetarian restaurant in the city for South Indian specialities, and also for Punjabi dishes, *tandoori* and delicious *dosas*. *In Hotel Arya Nivas, right at the station | tel. 0471 2 33 07 89 | Moderate*

KALAVARA
Amidst the bustle of Trivandrum this three-storey restaurant is like an oasis of calm. In addition to Indian and European dishes, the restaurant also specialises in Chinese cuisine. The best place to sit is under the sun umbrellas on the roof terrace. *Press Rd | tel. 0471 2 72 70 34 | Moderate*

SHOPPING

On the main shopping thoroughfare *MG*

Road you'll also find *Chalai Bazaar* and *Connemara Market,* where you can buy freshly caught fish (mornings only), fruit, vegetables and spices, as well as beautiful materials, gold jewellery and even bags and suitcases (bargaining essential).

SARWAA LIFESTYLE STORE ⚑

At Tigi Philip's there are ethnic products in rustic design made from natural materials, such as hand-block print fabrics, fine lin-

BEACHES IN THE VICINITY

KOVALAM BEACH (150 B6) (⚐ E13)
This is considered Kerala's most important beach, and lies 16 km/9.9 mi south of Trivandrum. Kovalam consists of a small town and a series of three connecting bays, Lighthouse, Hawah and Samudra, all characterised by their unusual rock formations. The southernmost section, *Lighthouse Beach,* is named

A different world south of Kerala's capital: Lighthouse Beach in Kovalam

gerie, jewellery and writing paper, decorative accessories – everything is eye-catching and made by young designers. Tigi encourages self-help groups for women to maintain traditional production methods. A café is also attached. *Sankar Rd, Althara Nagar, Sasthamangalam*

S. M. S. M. HANDICRAFT EMPORIUM

One of the best arts and crafts, jewellery and material shops – with fixed prices. *Puthenchanthai*

after the 35-m/114.8-ft high lighthouse on Kurumkal Hill. Many stalls selling colourful travellers' clothing, fast food and massage deals line *Hawah Beach* in particular. However, Lighthouse and Hawah beaches are no longer as clean as they once were. The recently renovated seafront promenade consists almost exclusively of shops and hotels, but you are compensated by the sight of fishermen pulling their boats up on the beach in the evenings.

One recommended hotel is *The Leela Kovalam (tel. 0471 2 48 01 01 | www.the leela.com | Expensive)*. This extensive complex with a total of 186 rooms is built on terraces leading down to the sea. It has two infinity pools, seven restaurants and a large spa. The *Thapovan Resort (Nellikunnu, Mulloor | tel. 0471 2 48 04 53 | www.thapovan.com | Moderate)* with its 31 rooms housed in small bungalows, stretches across a sloping garden down to Nellikunnu beach. It has made a reputation for itself as an Ayurveda resort. The ᴺᴵ₂ uppermost of its two restaurants offers a fantastic panoramic view of the sea. The owner will direct guests to local events, from the food festival in the neighbouring village to temple festivals; his excursions

LOW BUDGET

The cheapest and most exciting way to get to know Kerala and its inhabitants is through homestays, that is private accommodation. You can go on excursions, enjoy eating authentic food with local people and get their advice and tips. You can find addresses at local tourist offices or at *www. homestaykerala.org*.

Far cheaper than a houseboat is discovering the Backwaters *(see p. 75, 92)* by public ferry. They regularly ply between Alappuzha, Kollam and Kottayam. The 2½-hour journey between Alappuzha and Kottayam, for example, crosses Vembanad Lake, an important habitat for birds, and costs only 20 Rs. The public ferries operate daily from 7.30am to 5.15pm.

will not cost any more than the taxi journey. Meanwhile, the view from the ᴺᴵ₂ INSIDER TIP terrace of the *rockholm hotel (Lighthouse Rd, Vizhinja | tel. 0471 2 48 03 06 | www.rockholm.com | Moderate)* is priceless, with the lighthouse and the palm-lined bay below. Local speciality: *fish molee,* a fish curry with coconut rice. No alcohol. The trendiest restaurant is the *Fusion (Lighthouse Beach | tel. 0471 2 48 41 53 | Moderate),* which offers the choice of three cuisines: Eastern, Western and, naturally, Fusion – the combination of a variety of influences. There's always something going on in the evenings around the bars and restaurants on Kovalam's beach promenade. Good live music is played at the open-air *Beatles Restaurant (tel. 093 87 80 19 42 | Moderate)*. If you fancy some cakes, try the ᴺᴵ₂ *German Bakery (Lighthouse Beach | tel. 0471 2 48 01 79)* – especially for breakfast on the terrace. Although it's more like a restaurant than a bakery, you can get delicious cakes, waffles and pancakes there. The sea view is free.

VARKALA ★ ᴺᴵ₂ (150 B5) (*Ø E13*)
At the base of the red cliffs, *Panasam Beach* extends for just under a kilometre. It is much less crowded than Kovalam Beach. However, there's a certain clash of cultures in Varkala: on the one hand, the girls in bikinis who don't take much notice of the ban on topless sunbathing; on the other, the ● practising Hindus, who, early in the morning, at the southern end of the beach and in the presence of white-robed priests, hold ceremonies for their departed loved-ones, five days after their death, and then cast the consecrated ashes into the sea. Afterwards, they take a spiritually healing bath in the pool of the *Janardhanaswamy Temple*. Sixty steps lead up to the 2000-year-old temple, but non-Hindus are not allowed to enter its

Keeping hold of the catch: fishermen mending their nets on Varkala beach

sanctuary. For holidaymakers, backpackers and dropouts alike, the place to head for in Varkala is the ● 🌿 *Path on the Cliff*. Along this paved path there are hotels and guest houses one after another, colourful clothes blowing in the wind in front of the many shops and boutiques, Ayurveda offered at every corner and, in front of the bars, cafés and restaurants, chairs facing the sea ready for the sunset. The cliff path is being continually extended, so that further resorts can be built. After all, it's up here where you will find the best views, such as from the *Kerala Bamboo House (Papanasam Cliff, Kurakkani | tel. 098 95 27 09 93 | www.kerala bamboohouse.com | Budget)*, where 24 huts and an Ayurveda centre have been built entirely from materials found in the forest. Just one disadvantage: no hot water. At the *Akhil Beach Resort (Papanasam Cliff | tel. 0470 2 60 09 42 | www.akhilbeachresort.com | Moderate)* the eleven deluxe cottages and the six rooms in the main building are surround-ed by a pleasant garden; they also offer Ayurveda, yoga and meditation.

Beneath the cliff, right on the south beach, lies the 🌿 *Hindustan Beach Retreat (Papanasam Beach | tel. 0470 2 60 42 54 | www.hindustanbeachretreat. com | Moderate)*, which also serves as accommodation for pilgrims. Here too, there are great views of the sea from the rooftop restaurant and all 27 rooms and three suites. There's also a pool, as well as Ayurveda treatments and yoga. A little way away from the beach, the *Eden Garden Ayurvedic Retreat (Papanasam Beach | tel. 094 47 77 79 37 | www. edengarden.in | Budget–Moderate)* offers a wide range of treatments. The red houses with twelve rooms are situated under palm trees and by a fish pond. *50 km/31.1 mi northwest*

ENTERTAINMENT

NEERA BAR 🌿
The best thing about this bar is the

incredible view of the sea. But they also mix good cocktails, have a wide selection of wines and serve sushi and tapas. There's only room for about 30 people, and the lounge atmosphere is enhanced by appropriate music and bar billiards. Smokers congregate on the adjacent terrace. *Daily 11am–10pm | Kovalam, Vivanta by Taj Hotel, G.V. Raja Vattappara Rd | tel. 0471 6 61 30 00*

WHERE TO STAY

HOTEL HYCINTH
The chic new 4-star hotel with 104 rooms is in the heart of the town. Its highlight its the large outdoor pool on the roof terrace, where barbeques with live music are held in the evenings. *Manorama Rd, Thampanoor | tel. 0471 3 31 29 99 | hycinthhotels.com | Moderate*

NANDANAM PARK
This new hotel is nice and bright, with clean lines throughout. It has 32 rooms, two restaurants and an airy ⚘ rooftop café, which has views over the city. A modern establishment, it lies in the heart of the city, a kilometre or so from the station. *Nandavanam Rd, opposite the A. R. Police Camp, Palayam | tel. 085 90 90 16 11 | www.nandanampark.com | Budget*

RESIDENCY TOWER
This white building in the heart of the city is reminiscent of Miami. The 63 rooms are bright and modern, and there's a pool as well as a rooftop restaurant. *Press Rd | tel. 0471 2 33 16 61 | www.residencytower.com | Moderate*

INFORMATION

TOURIST INFORMATION CENTRE
Park View, next to the museum | tel. 0471 2 32 11 32 | www.keralatourism.org

TOURIST FACILITATION CENTRE
In the Guest House Compound, next to the bus station, Kovalam | tel. 0471 2 48 00 85

WHERE TO GO

KOLLAM (QUILON) ★
(150 B5) (*Ⓜ D12*)
Kollam (pop. 361,000) lies between the sea and the 16-km/9.9-mi long Ashtamudi Lake, the gateway to the Backwaters. The architecture is characterised by typical Keralan wooden houses with red-tile roofs. Kollam is also famous for the processing of cashew nuts, and large houseboats are built in the Alumkadavu boatyard. In many places in town, coconut fibres are made into mats and ropes. Situated nearby is the famous *Amritapuri Ashram* (see p. 24) of Mata Amritanandamayi *(tel. 0476 2 89 75 78 | www.amritapuri.org)*.

KONNI (150 B5) (*Ⓜ E12*)
Around 68 km/42.3 mi north of Thiruvananthapuram, near Pathanamthitta, lies the small settlement of Konni. For animal lovers it's worth making the trip on account of the *Elephant Training Centre (daily 10am–5.30pm | 60 Rs)*. Established as long ago as 1941, it is the oldest in India. Pachyderms that have been abandoned by the herd or found wounded are accommodated in enormous wooden stables. Visitors can watch them bathing in the Achankovil River and also try their hand at riding. Recently, a butterfly museum has been installed at the camp. Just one kilometre away lies the elegant *Contour Jungle Resort (tel. 0468 2 24 97 49 | www.contourjungle.com | Expensive)*, which has 14 rooms in cottages.

NEYYAR WILDLIFE SANCTUARY
(150 B–C6) (*Ⓜ E13*)
With its varied terrain of rushing streams,

slopes and meadows, this game park is ideal for trekking with an ascent of up to 1868 m/6129 ft to the high *Agashthyamala Peak* (3–4 hours depending on fitness). Trekking permits are issued by the *Kerala Forestry & Wildlife Department*, but only in January/February. In the jungle-like park, which covers 46 mi² around the Neyyar dam lake, you can see elephants, muntjac and mountain goats. *Admission 50 Rs, Jeep safaris 250 Rs per jeep plus 10 Rs for the guide | Information office at the entrance, more information: The Forestry Warden (Trivandrum | tel. 0471 2 36 07 62). 30 km/18.6 mi east*

PONMUDI (150 B6) (*E13*)
This idyllic hill station lies 61 km/37.9 mi northeast of Trivandrum at a height of 915 m/3002 ft. It is the perfect place for extended, easy walks past bubbling springs and wild orchids. There are also numerous winding paths meandering through tea and rubber plantations. One of them leads to the *Meenmutti waterfall,* 15 km/9.3 mi away, where the *Kallar River* plunges into the depths. Recommended accommodation is the *KTDC Golden Peak Resort (tel. 0472 2 89 02 25 | Budget)* with its 14 rooms in small cottages with eco-roofs. It lies in a garden among wooded hills.

POOVAR ISLAND (150 B6) (*E13*)
This paradise island lies between the Backwaters and the open sea. Even though boats cross to the offshore sandbar, swimming in the sea is not allowed because of the strong current. In return, you have two resorts that offer maximum relaxation in complete seclusion, both specialising in Ayurveda. In addition, the *Poovar Island Resort (tel. 0471 2 21 20 68 | www.poovarislandresort. com | Moderate)* has its very own dentist so you can catch up on your dental care. Spread across an area of 62 acres are villas housing 78 rooms, as well as 16 overwater bungalows. Also: two pools,

In a rubber plantation near Ponmudi

beauty salon, no cars, no plastic, biogas, solar power. Green Leaf certification.
On the neighbouring property stands the *Estuary Island Resort (tel. 0471 2 56 10 12 | www.thrhotels.com | Moderate)*, spread across 37 acres with 71 rooms in cottages and a three-storey main building. They also have a pool and Ayurveda centre. *12 km/7.5 mi south*

BACKWATERS

Kerala's real highlights are the ★ *Backwaters*, a network of around 1900 km/1180 mi of canals, which at certain points expand into large lakes. The district of *Alappuzha* (Alleppey) is regarded as the 'Venice of Kerala'. That's where the large ● houseboats are moored; modelled on the old rice boats, they are made of wood and tied together with coconut fibres. The main routes run between *Kollam* (Quilon) and Alappuzha, the principal centre of Backwater tours. To get a taste, you can take one of the public ferries (see p. 88).

Just a relatively short trip on a motorboat will give you a good impression of the magical, watery world of the Backwaters, with its stunning flora and fauna. Sometimes, they widen into large lakes like Ashtamudi, Kayamkulam and Vembanad. And sometimes, such as at Trikunnipuzha, the canals get so narrow that you can reach out and touch the palm leaves on the bank.

The Backwaters run like arteries through villages, rice fields and palm groves. Canoes, loaded with vegetables, *tapioca*, areca and cashew nuts, regularly cross the path of the tour boats. Waving children will often run after the boats along the banks. Stretched between the palm trees, you'll also see ropes, on which the *toddy tapper* balances as he taps the freshly fermented coconut juice. The house- and motorboats usually stop at one of the small *toddy bars* so you can have a taste, together with a piece of grilled *karimeen,* the local Backwaters fish. Chanting emanates from Hindu temples and thousands of migrating birds perch in the trees.

HOUSEBOAT TOURS

Today's houseboats are converted *kettuvalloms,* cargo boats that once transported people and material, rice and spices to Kochi harbour. *Kettu* means to sew, *vallom* means boat; the boat builders use only wood and coconut twine, not a single nail. Navigating the narrow canals requires considerable skill, and long poles are often deployed. With several closed cabins, shower/WC, dining area and sun deck, the converted boats offer tourists lots of comfort. You can sail through the backwaters for several days; a cook will look after the catering. Recent years have seen a considerable increase in the number of houseboats

Life on the water: simply go with the flow along a labyrinth of delightful lakes and canals

on the Backwaters, and now there are over a thousand of them, run by more than 50 operators. For laymen, it is not easy to tell the differences in quality. Either book a tour from home through a specialist operator, go through a good agent in India, or the *Tourist Office* in Alappuzha or Kollam. To be on the really safe side you can also think about arranging a tour through a good hotel that has its own houseboat.

DAY TRIPS

A day trip with a houseboat costs about 6500 Rs for 2 people, 10,000 Rs for a 2-person luxury houseboat. You can book, for example, with a large operator such as ☻ *Rainbow Cruises (tel. 0477 2 23 11 10 | www.rainbowcruises. in)*, which, like some other companies, tries to increase environmental awareness among the villagers. For a ride on a motorboat, expect to pay approx. 350 Rs per person per hour.

Kollam–Alappuzha tours commence daily at 10.30am from the pier, trips to the villages aboard a *country boat* are offered daily between 9am–1pm and 2pm–6pm. Information: *DTPC Tourist Information Office | KSRTC Bus Stand, Kollam*

There are also daily tours running in the opposite direction, from Alappuzha to Kollam: the Backwater Cruise takes eight hours and costs 300 Rs per person *(10.30am from DTPC pier)*; from Alappuzha to Kumarakom it leaves from the DTPC pier daily at 11am *(150 Rs, minimum 10 people)*. Or you can hire a rowing boat to tour the villages *(150 Rs per hr/person)*. Information: *The Administrative Office DTPC (by the pier, Alappuzha | tel. 0477 2 25 33 08 | www.dtpc alappuzha.com)* or *Tourist Reception Centre DTPC (by the KSRTC bus station, Kollam | tel. 0474 2 25 17 96)*.

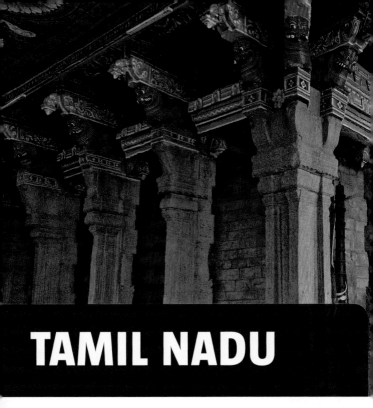

TAMIL NADU

Tamil Nadu, a world of wonder: this magical mix of nature and culture, of beaches, green hill stations and historical sites, has always enthralled travellers. Clocks work differently here, notions of time matter less.

Magnificent temples adorn every village. In Madurai the temple contains amazingly decorated entrance towers, or *gopuram,* the sea temples in Mamallapuram are subject to the laws of eternal wave action. Tamil Nadu can also boast of having the most World Heritage Sites. Three of the five sites are located in Thanjavur, the other two in Chennai and Nilgiri.

Even in prehistoric times, people were settling in the area of the present-day state of Tamil Nadu, which emerged out of the province of Madras in 1969. With an area of just over 50,000 mi² the state is about the same size as Greece. The art and culture of this region are among the oldest in the world. One of the world's longest surviving classical languages, the Tamil language was written down 5000 years ago and first spoken long before that. Tamil Nadu can be regarded as one of the last remaining places on earth with a continuing classical culture. The ancient Dravidian heritage is still very much alive; history doesn't just refer to the dim distant past, but it lives on in music and dance, in the palaces and temples where ancient beliefs continue to be practised.

Since time immemorial, each day has begun with women, in front of their houses, painting kolams – intricate styl-

Sea temples and hill stations, ancient cultures and beautiful landscapes offer a unique range of attractions

ised patterns made with coloured rice powder. This strong sense of creativity manifested in the film industry, for which the state is famous. 'There's more to cinema than Bollywood', they say. Outsized movie posters of film heroes and heroines adorn the walls of houses in every town, in every village. And the refined culture of Tamil Nadu has even left its mark on the cuisine. Among connoisseurs, the region of Chettinad is considered the home of India's gourmet chefs, its cuisine incorporating a varie-ty of culinary influences from across the continent. Delicious, delicately spiced dishes of mutton, chicken and fish are prepared here, and the art of making excellent coffee has been perfected.

To enjoy the pleasures of high society, the British colonial masters took to their chic *hill stations* like Ooty, also known as Udhagamandalam. Today's influx will discover an amazing amount to see and do: surrounded by the Bay of Bengal with its palm-lined beaches in the east, the Nilgiri Mountains (part of

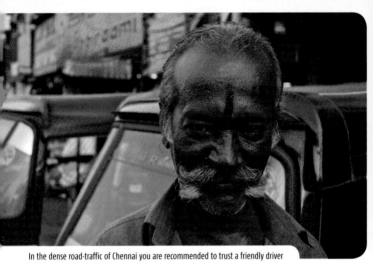

In the dense road-traffic of Chennai you are recommended to trust a friendly driver

the Western Ghats) in the west, the Indian Ocean in the south and the Deccan Plateau in the north, Tamil Nadu offers lots of variety. When not on the palm beaches plunging into the temptingly warm waters of the Indian Ocean, active holidaymakers go trekking, fishing, canoeing, or play golf. While the total of 900 km/560 mi of beaches along Tamil Nadu's Coromandel Coast might not be as well-known as those in Goa or Kerala, they do have their own special character. Much was destroyed by the 2004 tsunami, but there's little evidence of that disaster today. Had it occurred 2000 years ago it would have been carved in stone for all eternity – just like so many other events in Tamil Nadu's history.

CHENNAI (MADRAS)

 MAP INSIDE BACK COVER
(149 F4) (*H8*) **The climate in and around Tamil Nadu's capital, Chennai (pop. 4.9 million), is described as 'hot, hotter, the hottest'.**

That may be something of an exaggeration, as in the Bay of Bengal it 'only' gets as warm as 32 °C/90 °F. Alongside the booming IT sector, the city once called Madras, the fourth-largest metropolis in India, can be proud of a history stretching back almost 2000 years. A vivid example of this rich past is the district of *Mylapore*. Beside the Hindu temple of Kapaleeshwarar and Chennai's oldest place of Christian worship, Luz Church, stands the Basilica San Thome – one of three churches worldwide said to contain the grave of one of the Twelve Apostles. An equally exciting mixture of temples, churches and colonial buildings such as the High Court and the imposing Post Office, thrives in the business district of *George Town*. While Mumbai is well ahead as a producer of Bollywood movies, Chennai has made a big name for itself as the centre of the Tamil film industry – 'Kollywood' as they call it.

WHERE TO START?
Government Museum in Egmore: At *Egmore Railway Station* and near the bus terminals is the Government Museum. From here, buses of the *Metropolitan Transportation Corporation (www.mtcbus. org)* nos. 10 and 11 will take you right through the city, and are extremely cheap. The MTC also goes to Fort St George at Marina Beach, to San Thome Basilica and the neighbouring Kapaleeshwarar Temple.

SIGHTSEEING

FORT ST GEORGE
This stately fortress is very well preserved. Dating from the 17th century, it was originally built by the Portuguese and later protected the British trading outpost of Chennai. The white fort also contains the oldest Anglican church in India, *St Mary's*, which was built in 1680. Displays inside the *Fort Museum* include interesting exhibits from the time of the East India Company: uniforms, weapons and medals. In the neighbouring cemetery stand the oldest British gravestones in India. *Sat–Thu 9.30am–5pm | 100 Rs | Kamarajar Salai | south George Town*

GOVERNMENT MUSEUM CHENNAI
With its palace-like main building, this red-coloured museum is one of the oldest in the country. It consists of a total of six buildings dotted around a park, each one devoted to a different theme. The site is also home to the *National Art Gallery,* the *Contemporary Art Gallery,* the *Bronze Gallery* and the *Museum of Childhood. Sat–Thu 9.30am–5pm | 250 Rs, camera 200 Rs, video 500 Rs | Pantheon Rd, Egmore | www.chennaimuseum.org*

HORTICULTURAL GARDEN
A wonderfully green, cool oasis in the heart of the city is the 22-acre garden – also known as Semmohi Poonga. It

★ **Kapaleeshwarar Temple**
This temple of Shiva in Chennai has a splendid, colourful *gopuram* → p. 98

★ **Fisherman's Cove**
A smart resort on the picture-postcard Covelong Beach → p. 101

★ **Mamallapuram**
Amazing place with sea temples, caves and beautiful rock reliefs → p. 103

★ **Puducherry**
The white city exudes French charm → p. 104

★ **Sri Meenakshi Temple**
Twelve *gopuram* and a total of 33 million figures adorn South India's largest temple complex in Madurai. It's worth staying to see the night ceremony → p. 106

★ **Rock Fort**
Like a swallow's nest, castle and temple cling to their rocky eyrie high above Tiruchirappalli → p. 110

★ **Udhagamandalam**
Very British: with its English architecture, Ooty or Ootacamund was considered the Queen of hill stations → p. 110

MARCO POLO HIGHLIGHTS

is planted with rare trees, shrubs, bonsais and flowerbeds. *Fri–Wed 8.30am–12.30pm, 1.30pm–5.30pm | admission free | Cathedral Rd*

KAPALEESHWARAR TEMPLE ★

This temple to Shiva, full of sacred statues, including bronze effigies of the 63 Shaivate saints, boasts a splendid, colourful tower, the 37-m/121.4-ft high *gopuram*. The original temple, thought to date from the 7th century, was destroyed by the Portuguese; the present complex is only about 300 years old. Non-Hindus are welcome to step inside the temple courtyard. *Tue–Sun 5.30am–9pm | camera 200 Rs, video 500 Rs | North Mada St, Mylapore*

LUZ CHURCH

The oldest church in Chennai, also known as 'Our Dear Lady of Light' or 'Kaatu Kovil', was erected by Franciscans in 1516. It is said that once, when a ship got into difficulties during a storm, the crew saw a light on the shore that pointed the way to safety. Some years later, to give thanks, the Portuguese built a church at the same spot. *Luz Church Rd, Mylapore*

SAN THOME BASILICA (ST THOMAS MOUNT CHURCH)

One of three churches worldwide that was built over the grave of an apostle. St Thomas was buried here after his martyrdom, a small church was erected in 1523. Both this and a later church crumbled, and it wasn't until 1896 that the white cathedral was built; it was accorded the status of a basilica in the year 1956. In the crypt, a statue of the apostle lies in a glass coffin over the grave. *Daily 6am–8pm | Santhome High Rd, Mylapore | www.santhomechurch.com*

LOW BUDGET

You can eat well and cheaply in restaurants where there are no tables or chairs and you just have a plate in your hand. They are called *kaiyendhi bhavans* in Tamil Nadu and in Kerala they're known as *thattu kadai*. They usually serve typical South Indian snacks such as *idlis, dosas* and *puris*. You can eat at least as cheaply in the *dhabas*, simple roadside restaurants of North Indian origin. Their sweet *chai*, which is prepared over a charcoal fire, and *chicken tikka masala* (spiced chicken) are particularly popular.

You can get around cheaply in Puducherry. Large motor-rickshaws *(4-wheelers)* for max. 8 people stop everywhere on request.

In Mysore there are lots of ☺ cycle rickshaws. This environmentally friendly and cheap way of getting round all the sights or going from point A to point B also supports a dying profession.

The journey with the local train from the Chennai airport to the city centre only costs 10 Rs. Tirusulam train station is opposite the airport.

FOOD & DRINK

INSIDER TIP AMETHYST CAFÉ
This café belongs to a gallery full of antiquities, paintings and old photographs, housed in a lovely old villa. You eat outside in the garden among giant ferns and palm trees. The menu has mainly Italian dishes. A lovely, green oasis in the heart

Do you also sense a certain arrogance from the figure at Kapalishvara Temple? That's Gods for you!

of the city. *Padmavathi Rd | tel. 044 28 54 16 23 | www.amethystchennai.com | Moderate*

ANNALAKSHMI

Purely vegetarian, this restaurant is a project sponsored by the *Temple of Fine Arts International,* which combines art, cuisine, dance and theatre and so it also serves as a gallery of art and applied art. *18/3 Rukmani Lakshmipathy Rd, Egmore | tel. 044 28 52 51 09 | www.annalakshmi chennai.co.in | Expensive*

SARAVANABHAVAN

An affordable restaurant which serves up a good range of vegetarian dishes, both Chinese and South Indian; delicious *thalis* in particular. *Vadapalani Andavar, Koil St | tel. 044 24 80 25 77 | www.saravana bhavan.com | Budget*

SHOPPING

Chennai's main shopping areas are *Parry's Corner* and *Anna Salai.*

CENTRAL COTTAGE INDUSTRIES EMPORIUM

This state-run emporium for Indian arts and crafts, material, saris, jewellery and much more offers good quality at fixed prices. *672, Temple Towers, Anna Salai, Nandanam | www.cottageemporium.in*

PLANET M

Unbeatable prices in this shop, which is a real eldorado for all music and film fans. It has branches in other cities of South India, as well as three in Chennai: *3rd Ave Anna Nagar; 113 Kutchery Rd, Mylapore; A 9 Abirami, Mega Mall, Kilpauk*

SPORTS & ACTIVITIES

INSIDER TIP DANCE SHOWS

Bharatanatyam, a solo dance from Tamil Nadu, is one of eight classical Indian dance styles that by their form of expression relate certain religious episodes from Hindu mythology. The dance's roots lie in South Indian temple culture. There's an opportunity to watch students of Bharatanatyam by visiting the *Kalakshetra School of Dance. Mon–Fri 10–11.30am | 200 Rs | Kalaksheta Rd, Thiruvanmiyur | tel. 044 24 52 40 57 | www.kalakshetra.in*

BEACHES IN THE VICINITY

All beaches, from north to south (149 F4) (*M H8–9*)

MARINA BEACH

The city of Chennai's wide and 12-km/7.5-mi long beach stretches from Fort St George in the north to Velankanni Church in the south. Stone statues of famous politicians, including Mahatma Gandhi, line the coast road. A stroll along the beach will take in a number of colonial buildings such as the Senate House, the University Library and the Chepauk Palace. Swimming is not recommended as the water isn't clean enough.

ELLIOT'S BEACH

At the southern end of Marina Beach in Chennai, the curving Elliot's Beach has been used as a location for a number of Tamil films. The sand and water here are clean, the waves are perfect for surfers and there is a choice of restaurants for sustenance.

COVELONG BEACH

Visitors to this broad, palm-fringed beach, situated just 40 km/24.9 mi south of Chennai, can enjoy the added attraction of some small fishing villages – it's an almost untouched idyll. All that lies on the beautiful beach itself is the

Lift and eyes up!: the Kalakshetra School of Dance trains classical dancers

★ *Fisherman's Cove (Covelong Beach | tel. 044 67 41 33 33 | www.tajhotels.com | Expensive)*. It has 152 rooms, some in cottages, good yoga courses and, amongst other restaurants, the romantic *Bay View Point* right on the water's edge.

ENTERTAINMENT

When it comes to nightlife, Chennai has quite a lot to offer. However, all clubs and bars have to close by midnight so places open up correspondingly early.

BIKE & BARREL RESTOBAR

In this comfy pub/bar, beer is served straight from the barrel, and a 1946 Norton Classic motorcycle hangs from the ceiling. At weekends there is a dress code; anyone looking scruffy will be

turned away. *Daily 11am–0.30am | 115 Residency Towers | Sir Theagaraya Rd | www.theresidency.com*

PASHA

The best-known nightclub in the city is at the *Park Hotel*. A sultry, oriental atmosphere, hundreds of mirrors reflecting the dance floors and seating, cushions and candles. Admission for couples only. *1000 Rs | 601 Anna Salai | www.thepark hotels.com*

SATHYAM CINEMAS ●

Cinema in India is a thrilling experience. This multiplex in the centre has six different theatres, the largest of which seats 948 people; they show international movies as well as Hindi productions à la Bollywood, also in 3-D versions. In addition: vegetarian restaurant, amusement arcade. *8 Thiruvika Rd | tel. 044 42 24 42 24 | www. sathyamcinemas.com*

WHERE TO STAY

HOTEL PANDIAN

It hardly gets more central than this: in two minutes you're at the Egmore Railway Station, and the Central Railway Station is just a five-minute taxi ride away. The rooms are clean and quiet, the main sound being the call of the muezzin from the nearby mosque. Equipped with internet café *(daily 7am–11pm)*. *90 rooms | 15 Kenneth Lane, Egmore | tel. 044 28 19 10 10 | www.hotelpandian. com | Budget*

NEW VICTORIA

This hotel has 50 rooms, is just 200 m/656 ft from the station and offers excellent value for money. It has a restaurant serving international cuisine and a bar. *3 Kenneth Lane | tel. 044*

28 19 36 38 | www.empeehotels.com | Moderate

INSIDER TIP  NEW WOODLANDS HOTEL
The walls of this centrally located hotel are adorned with images of the Hindu epics. It has an outdoor pool, a beauty salon, two vegetarian restaurants (no alcohol), and is a favourite with international travellers. *175 rooms, some in cottages | 72–75 Dr Radhakrishnan Rd, Mylapore | tel. 044 28 11 31 11 | www.new woodlands.com | Budget–Moderate*

INFORMATION

Sightseeing tours through *Tamil Nadu Tourism Development Corporation (TTDC): half-day Chennai (daily 1.30pm–6.30pm) in air-conditioned bus | 375 Rs; day trip Chennai–Mamallapuram (daily 9am–7pm) with numerous stops (air-con. bus) | 625 Rs | fees for museums extra.* All tours start at *Tamil Nadu Tourism Complex | 2 Wallajah Rd | tel. 044 25 33 34 44 | www.tamilnadu tourism.org*

INDIA TOURISM CHENNAI
154 Anna Salai | tel. 044 28 46 02 85

WHERE TO GO

CHIDAMBARAM (149 E6) (*ſ H10*)
Like Madurai, the small city of Chidambaram (pop. 62,000) was built around its temple. Between 907 and 1310 this was the capital of the important Chola Empire. Today, it's mainly students from the Annamalai University who throng the streets and bustling market of the old city centre. The main attraction is the *Nataraja Temple (daily 6am–1pm and 4pm–10pm).* Dating from the 11th century, this 40-acre temple precinct with its 1000-columned hall, is venerated as one of the holiest shrines in South India. The roof is gilded, and the four *gopuram* soar to a height of 42 m/137.8 ft. It is said that the lamps on the towers aided mariners with navigation. Non-Hindus are allowed to enter the holy of holies. At noon and again at 6pm, Nataraja, the statue of the dancing Shiva, is carried around in a litter.

The *Hotel Saradharam (19 Venugopal Pillai St | tel. 094 42 59 14 75 | www. hotelsaradharam.co.in | Moderate)* has 45 spacious rooms, some with balcony or terrace. The *Grand Palace Stay (12 Railway Feeder Rd, opposite the station | tel. 04144 23 93 39 | www.grandpalacestay. com | Budget)* with its futuristic facade and small garden has just 21 rooms, two restaurants (one of them vegetarian), a bar and free internet. Information: *Tourist Office, Railway Station Rd | tel. 04144 23 87 39. 232 km/144 mi south*

INSIDER TIP DAKSHINACHITRA ●
(149 F4) (*ſ H8*)
Some 25 km/15.5 mi south of Chennai lies this model village with traditional houses from all over South India. Demonstrations of art and handicrafts offer a fascinating insight into daily life. You can have mehndi patterns applied to your hands and a parrot will tell your fortune. *Wed–Mon 10am–6pm | 250 Rs | East Coast Rd, Muttukadu | www.dakshi nachitra.net*

KANCHIPURAM (149 E4) (*ſ G9*)
Kanchipuram (pop. 220,000) is considered to have been an example for the fusion of different religions. Of the more than 1000 places of worship it once had, 126 still remain. The *Vaikuntha Perumal Temple* was built in the 7th century by the Pallava king Nandhivarman. Located in the temple tower are unique images of the Lord Vishnu, seated, standing and recumbent. Dating from the 8th century,

Just kidding: Krishna's Butterball is not so easy to move

the sandstone *Kailasanathar Temple* has a main central shrine with 58 small shrines surrounding it. Kanchipuram is famous for its high quality silk saris. It's well worth visiting the *Weaver's Service Center (Railway Station Rd)*.

Recommended accommodation includes the *MM Hotel (65 Nellukkara St | tel. 044 27227250 | www.mmhotels.com | Budget–Moderate)*: the 48 rooms are clean and nicely furnished and the restaurant is right next-door. With its 33 rooms, the *Baboo Surya Hotel (85 East Raja St | tel. 044 27222556 | www.hotelbaboosoorya. com | Budget–Moderate)* has been completely renovated. It offers varied cuisine, and cocktails are mixed at the bar. Information: *At the fort. 75 km/46.6 mi southwest*

MAMALLAPURAM (MAHABALIPU-RAM) ★ (149 F4) (*Ω H9*)

Just 55 km/34.2 mi south of Chennai, in the small town of the same name (pop. 13,400), lies the incomparable Unesco World Heritage Site of Mamallapuram.

The art of stonemasonry has been preserved here and all over town you can hear the sound of hammer and chisel. In order for the magic of this former capital of the Pallava kings and their temple to fully sink in, you need to take your time. It is best to hire a bicycle *(100 Rs per day)*. The *Sea Shore Temple (500 Rs incl. rathas)* dating from the 7th century with its twin shrines stands majestically over the shore. Several temples were hewn into a 500-m/1640-ft long cliff. Because of its realistic depictions in the hall of pillars, the *Krishna Mandapam* temple is the most authentic. The five temple chariots, *rathas*, were hewn as monoliths from a single stone block, although they have no wheels. Among the chariots stands a life-sized stone elephant. *Arjuna's Penance* is the largest bas-relief in the world (27 × 9 m/89.6 x 29.5 ft) — full of elephants, celestial beings and people. *Krishna's Butterball* was created by nature. This giant block of granite weighing many tons seems to defy the laws of gravity by not rolling down the steep incline on which it is perched. Because of its relaxing atmosphere, international airline crews like to stay at the INSIDER TIP *Ideal Beach Resort (East Coast Rd, Devenera Village | tel. 044 24 49 51 61 | www.idealresort.com | Moderate)*. Its white/red villas with a total of 68 rooms stand in a large garden, together with an Ayurveda centre, beauty salon, tennis courts and pool. The 72 bright rooms at the ❄ Sea Breeze *(Ottawadai St | tel. 044 27 44 30 35 | www.hotelsea breeze.in | Budget–Moderate)* might be basic, but the hotel has beautiful views of the Shore Temple. It also has a pool, garden restaurant and Ayurveda centre. Information: *Tourist Information | Kovalam Rd, adjacent to the police station | tel. 044 27 44 22 32*

MANGROVE PICHAVARAM FOREST ●
(151 F2) (*ΜΨ G10*))

Away from civilisation, a boat ride takes you through the mangroves. The *Pichavaram Forest*, 13 km/8.1 mi east of Chidambaram, covers an area of 4.25 mi^2 and is, after Sundarbans (near Calcutta), the second largest mangrove forest in the world. It provides a habitat for a variety of birds including cormorants, storks, ibis and pelicans; a total of 144 species have been identified. Motorboat and rowing boat tours are offered (someone else does the rowing). *Tours lasting 2, 4 and 6 hours | from 1000 Rs | Tourist Office Chidambaram | Railway Feeder Rd | Boat Dept. | tel. 04144 23 87 39*

PUDUCHERRY (PONDICHERRY) ★
(151 F1) (*ΜΨ G–H 9–10*)

This city (pop. 1,200,000) is divided into two by a canal. On one side stand modern, ordinary-looking buildings, on the other the 'White City', which exudes a charm befitting the former capital of French India. Just 8 km/5 mi to the south, the secluded *Paradise Beach* can be reached by boat across a small river from Chunnambar Resort. Along the seafront promenade of *Goubert Salai* the great statesman Mahatma Gandhi is honoured with a 4-m/13.1-ft high statue.

Puducherry, the former capital of French-India, still evokes decorative, colonial charm

The *Puducherry Government Museum (Tue–Sun 9am–5pm)* in St Louis Street displays a collection of rare bronze and stone sculptures from the Pallava and Chola dynasties, as well as the bed of the governor general, François Dupleix.

In ● *La Boutique d'Auroville (Jawaharlal Nehru St.)* you can buy lovely things to prepare for INSIDER TIP *Auroville (www.auroville.org | 10 km/6.2 mi north of Puducherry)* and the *Sri Aurobindo Ashram*, which relocated to St. Gilles Street in Puducherry after the death of Mira Alfassa (1878–1973). Auroville, a large spiritual community, was established in 1968 by "The Mother" – Mira Alfassa – as successor of the philosopher Sri Aurobindo. Her vision was to have a universal city of spiritual freedom that could accommodate 50,000 people. Now, around 2400 people from 40 countries live on the 413-acre site of Auroville. In Ashram there are 1500 members, including 250 foreigners. Auroville's focal point is the 29-m/95.1-ft high *Matri Mandir*, a meditation centre beneath a golden dome. At the *Visitor's Centre (daily 9am–5pm | tel. 0413 2 62 26 11)* you can also find out about yoga courses and investigate the options for accommodation. Included almost everywhere in the price from about 500 Rs: laundry, bicycle hire and board. More information: *Puducherry | 40 Goubert Ave (coast road) | tel. 0413 2 33 94 97*

On the coast road, in the heart of the French quarter, is the hotel *The Promenade (38 rooms | 23 Goubert Ave | tel. 0413 2 22 77 50 | www.thepromenadepondicherry.com | Moderate–Expensive)* with modern design behind a colonial façade. Not altogether conventional accommodation is at ✪ *The Dune Eco Beach Village & Spa (Pudhukuppam, Keelputhupet | tel. 093 64 45 54 40 | www.duneecogroup.com | Moderate)*, approx. 15 km/9.3 mi from Puducherry.

This artists' village on the 700-m/2297-ft long beach with 55 bungalows (incl. bicycle) has a pool, an organic farm, tennis court and spa with Ayurveda and yoga. *165 km/103 mi south*

MADURAI

(151 D4) *(ℳ F11)* **Everything in this 2500-year-old city (pop. 1.2 million) on the Vaigai River revolves around the Sri Meenakshi Temple complex.**

The street plan of Madurai is aligned with the temple *gopuram*. Modest, new buildings contrast sharply with the opulent splendour of the religious complex, but the sweet aroma that wafts through the city provides enough in the way of compensation: Madurai is famous for its jasmine flowers, which are offered for sale on every street corner. In the Old Town, the narrow alleyways, the bazaar and the pedestrian zone are always a hive of activity. Even as capital of the Pandya Dynasty, who ruled from here for almost a thousand years until the 10th century, Madurai was both a thriving commercial centre and seat of three literary academies.

SIGHTSEEING

GANDHI MEMORIAL MUSEUM
This museum is dedicated to the great philosopher and freedom fighter Mahatma Gandhi (1869–1948). Besides a large photographic exhibition on his life, numerous anti-British writings are on display. Other exhibits include some of Gandhi's few personal belongings, such as the blood-spattered *dhoti* he was wearing when assassinated. *Daily 10am–1pm and 2–5.30pm | free admission, camera 50 Rs | Rani Mangammal Palace | www.gandhimmm.org*

SRI MEENAKSHI SUNDARESHWARAR TEMPLE ★

Considered the biggest architectural marvel in all South India, this temple is dedicated to Lord Shiva in his incarnation as *Sundareshwarar* and his wife Parvati in her incarnation as *Meenakshi*. Visible from afar, the four *gopuram*, which soar up to 46 m/151 ft in height, dominate the city. There is actually a total of 12 *gopuram* within the temple precinct; the renovated towers are adorned with an unbelievable number of colourful deities and demons, said to number some 33 million in all. Since it was first erected in 1560, the complex in Madurai's Old Town has continuously expanded to the size it is today, namely 16 acres. It is considered a perfect example of Dravidian architecture. A particular highlight is the 1000-columned hall. Next door is an art museum containing statues of all the Hindu gods. For non-Hindus there is no admission to the Meenakshi shrine. During the nightly *Arathi Ceremony* between 9 and 9.30pm the statue of Shiva is carried through the temple on a silver litter to join Parvati. *Daily 5am–12.30pm and 4pm–9.30pm | 50 Rs, admission to art museum 5 Rs | camera and video not allowed | www.maduraimeenakshi.org*

THIRUMALAI NAYAK PALACE

Located about 1.5 km/0.9 mi from the Meenakshi Temple, this palace was built in 1636 for the ruler Thirumalai Nayak. An imposing building, it is renowned for the richly carved decoration in its dome and arches, as well as for its enormous 20-m/65.6-ft high white columns. The *Swargavilasa* (Celestial Pavilion) measures 75 × 52 m/246.1 x 170.6 ft, its central dome floating 25 m/82 ft above the floor. A sound & light show *(in English at 6.45pm)* brings Thirumalai Nayak, one of the most popular Madurai kings, back to life. *Daily 9am–1pm and 2pm–5pm | 50 Rs | camera/video 100 Rs*

FOOD & DRINK

ANNA MEENAKSHI

Vegetarian restaurant with a very reasonably priced menu, including delicious *thalis* authentically served on banana leaves. *West Perumal Maistry St | tel. 0452 4 37 29 00 | Budget*

PARK PLAZA ROOF TERRACE ☆

From the hotel's newly renovated rooftop terrace (seating for about 60 guests) you can enjoy the panoramic view of the temple's four gopurams – especially romantic in the evenings! The speciality is the oven-baked *tandoori*, besides there are also numerous – also vegetarian – dishes. *114–115 West Perumal Maistry St./corner of West Mada St. | tel. 0452 3 01 11 11 | Moderate*

SURYA

The Surya Restaurant serves vegetarian, Indian-Chinese dishes and from its ☆ roof terrace you can also enjoy priceless views of the illuminated Meenakshi Temple. *Approx. 10 min from the temple by auto-rickshaw, Hotel Supreme | 110 West Perumal Maistry St | tel. 0452 2 34 31 51 | www.hotelsupreme. in | Moderate*

SHOPPING

Madurai is famous for its cotton fabrics. Especially reasonable are the cotton saris, which are sold here in an unbelievable range of colours and patterns.

PUDUMANDAPAM MARKET ●

In the covered bazaar opposite the eastern entrance to the Meenakshi Temple, there are stalls selling lovely souvenirs

Washing amid the aquatic plants – it's just routine for locals in Chettinad

such as books, essential oils, cushion covers and shawls. Around INSIDER TIP 250 skilled tailors will guarantee completion of your made-to-measure garment within one hour. The best thing to do is order before your temple visit and collect the finished article afterwards. *Shop No. 126, Vijaya Stores* and *Shop No. 131, S. M. Tex* for example turn out particularly good quality items very rapidly.

WHERE TO STAY

HOTEL CHENTOOR

One of the most popular budget hotels with 48 neatly furnished rooms, some with balcony, it is located just ten minutes away from the temple. There are great views from the ☀ rooftop *Emperor Restaurant*. *106 West Perumal Maistry St | tel. 0452 3 07 77 77 | www.hotelchentoor.in | Budget*

GRT REGENCY

This modest business hotel is centrally located, very clean, has 57 functional rooms, a glass external lift and a fine restaurant with good cuisine. *38 Madakkulam Rd | tel. 0452 2 37 11 55 | www.grthotels.com/madurai | Moderate*

INSIDER TIP HERITAGE MADURAI

A genuine insider's tip is the approximately 150-year-old estate (17 acres) with 72 rooms. The stylish villas have understated elegance. It is 4 km/2.5 mi from the centre and has a pool, tennis court, badminton and Ayurveda spa. High quality at an affordable price! *11 Melakkal Main Rd, Kochadai | tel. 0452 2 38 54 55 | www.heritagemadurai.com | Moderate–Expensive*

INFORMATION

TOURIST INFORMATION

1 West Veli St | more counters at the airport and train station | tel. 0452 2 33 47 57

WHERE TO GO

CHETTINAD (151 D–E4) *(Ø F–G11)*
In fact, this area comprises a collection of 74 villages, located between

80 km/49.7 mi and 130 km/81 mi east of Madurai.

Relatively little visited, it is still considered as something of an insider tip. Within this small area, there is an astonishing concentration of palatial houses and mansions, built in the 19th century by wealthy local bankers and businessmen. On account of its numerous different influences, the famed Chettinad cuisine is regarded as the most aromatic and refined in all India. Craftsmen working in the pretty villages still create authentic handicrafts. In the region's largest town, *Karaikudi* (pop. 300,000), it is possible to visit a sari weaving centre, and in *Athangudi* you can watch the production of wonderful tiles at *Sri Ganesh Flower Tiles (A. Muthuppattinam, Sivaganga | tel. 04565 28 17 75)*. Many of the mansions can be visited. Some of them have evolved into beautiful hotels, such as the *Visalam (Local Fund Rd | LF Rd, Kanadukathan | tel. 04565 27 33 54 | www.cghearth.com/visalam | Expensive)* with 15 rooms, each over 1000 ft², and a pool. The chef Pandiyamma spoils guests with her Chettinad specialities. Not far from here, the *Chettinadu Palace (daily 10am–6pm | free admission | 11 AR St, Kanadukathan)* is famous for its teak columns and antiques. Functional, clean and reasonably priced, the *Udhayam* hotel, centrally located at the Sivagangai bus stop in Karaikudi *(Krishna Arcade, A-33 Sekkalai Rd | tel. 04565 23 40 68 | www.hoteludhayam.in | Budget)*, has 86 en-suite rooms.

KANYAKUMARI (CAPE COMORIN)
(150 C6) (*M E13*)

At the southernmost point of the subcontinent, where the Arabian Sea meets the Indian Ocean, lies Cape Comorin (pop. 23,000), a town known for its spectacular sunrises and sunsets.

The entire area is also an important pilgrimage destination. Here, in 1948, a temple to Mahatma Gandhi was erected, the *Gandhi Mandapam*. And on the exact day of Gandhi's birthday, 2 October, the sun's rays fall on the spot where the urn containing the Mahatma's ashes was kept for public viewing before immersion. On a rocky island, 500 m/1640 ft offshore, the spiritual leader and philosopher Swami Vivekananda meditated uninterrupted from 25 to 27 December 1892. A ferry *(daily 8am–4pm | 54 Rs)* will take you out there to see the memorial to the swami, as well as to another small island where an enormous statue of the poet Thiruvalluvar (c. 200 BC) stands.

Also right in the south, the beautiful, almost deserted sandy bay of INSIDER TIP *Vattakotai Beach*, 6 km/3.7 mi northeast of Kanyakumari, is still a real hidden gem with its calm water and dense palm grove. There is a lovely view over the sickle-shaped bay from the 18th-century ✹ *Vattakottai Fort*. The spiritually-oriented *Vivekananda Kendra Rest House (100 rooms | Vivekanandapuram | tel. 04652 24 62 50 | www.vivekanadakendra.org | Budget)* has a large garden and free shuttle bus service to the town 2 km/1.2 mi away. *242 km/150 mi southwest*

RAMESHWARAM BEACH
(151 E5) (*M G12*)

The sacred island of Rameshwaram with the temples of *Ramalingeshwaram*, *Gandhamandana Parvatam* and *Nambunayagi Amman Kali*, is located 163 km/101 mi southeast of Madurai. It can be reached via a bridge. Its gently shelving beaches are lined with palm trees and are deserted, apart from local fishermen. The shallow, clear water is perfect for swimming and snorkelling.

THANJAVUR (TANJORE)
(151 E3) (*G10*)

Situated in the fertile Kaveri Delta, the former capital of the Chola Empire (pop. 223,000) is now surrounded by rice paddies. Even today it boasts up to 90 temples. Among the most impressive is the 10th-century *Brihadeeswarar Temple (daily 6.30am–8.30pm),* a Unesco World Heritage Site. Constructed of red sandstone, the *gopuram* is an astonishing 72 m/236.2 ft high, and the Nandi Bull is almost 6 m/19.7 ft long and weighs 25 tons. The *Saraswati Mahal Library (Tue–Thu 10am–1pm and 1.30pm–5.30pm | Palace Campus | www.sarasvatimahalli brary.tn.nic.in),* which was installed in the *Thanjavur Palace* around 1700, is considered the most important historic library of the subcontinent. In addition to oriental and European works by poets and rulers, it contains more than 44,000 palm leaves inscribed with medical prescriptions and diagnoses in Sanskrit and Old Tamil. Behind the mighty walls of the *Thanjavur Royal Palace*, which dates from around 1550 *(daily 9.30am–1.30pm and 3pm–5pm | 10 Rs, camera 50 Rs, art gallery in the palace 30 Rs),* impressive frescoes, an underground tunnel and the splendid *Durbar Hall,* the former reception hall of the king, feature amongst the highlights. For accommodation in the city, try the *Parisutham (55-G A Canal Rd | tel. 04362 23 18 01 | www.hotelparisutham. com | Expensive).* With a location next to the canal, this modern hotel is laid out on terraces, has a lovely outdoor pool, an Ayurveda centre and 53 tastefully furnished rooms. Just 1 km/0.6 mi outside Thanjavur and beside a stream that flows between rice fields, the new *Paradise Resort (3/1216 Tanjore Main Rd, Darasuram, Ammapet, Kumabakonam | tel. 0435 2 41 64 69 | www.paradise resortindia.com | Moderate)* consists of small bungalows with a total of 52 rooms, all furnished with antiques from the surrounding villages. The restaurant is in the 200-year-old main

Lovely country houses, wonderful cuisine: Lakshmi seems well disposed towards Chettinad's main town of Karaikudi

building, but you can also dine in tree houses. Such a peaceful location is perfect for an Ayurveda cure. Information: *Hotel Tamil Nadu Complex, Gandhiji Rd | tel. 04362 23 09 84. 158 km/98 mi northeast*

TIRUCHIRAPPALLI (TRICHY)
(151 E3) *(🕮 G11)*
Situated to the north of Madurai, this green city (pop. 1,022,000) lies on the Kaveri River. Towering on a rocky outcrop 5 km/3.1 mi outside the town, the 83-m/272.3-ft high ★ *Rock Fort* is crowned by the *Ucchi Pillayar Temple (daily 6am–8pm | camera 20 Rs, video 100 Rs)*. The rocks are said to be approx. 3.8 billion years old. Climbing to the fortress takes you up 417 steps; on the way are small cave temples dating from the 7th century. But the view is worth all the effort. Some 6 km/3.7 mi north of Tiruchirappalli, the legendary temple city of *Srirangam* is spread across a nearly 1-mi² island that is surrounded by two rivers – the Kaveri and the Kollidam. The *Sri Ranganathaswamy Temple (daily 6.15am–1pm and 3.15pm–8.45pm | camera 50 Rs, video 200 Rs, tower ascent 10 Rs)* dates from between the 14th and 17th century and with its 21 *gopuram*, is one of the largest in India. Dedicated to the Lord Vishnu it is an important centre of pilgrimage. It also boasts seven courtyards and an imposing 1000-columned hall. Adjacent, the *Jambukeshwara Temple (daily 6am–1pm and 4pm–9.30pm | camera 20 Rs, video 150 Rs)* is just as old though considerably smaller, with only seven *gopuram*. Remember that non-Hindus are not allowed in the holy of holies. The temple is built around a *Shiva lingam* that stands in a sacred spring.

Shoulder ride in the temple city of Srirangam

Highly original with contemporary designer interiors is the *Hotel Sri Swarna Palace (75 B/2 North East Extension, Salai Rd, Thillainagar | www.hotelshriswarnaspalace.com | Budget)*. Special rooms available for female travellers. Prices at the 4-star hotel *Sangam (90 rooms | Collector's Office Rd | tel. 0431 2 41 47 00 | www.sangam hotels.com | Moderate)* are higher, but then it has a health club and pool among its facilities. Information: *Tourist Information Centre | Railway Junction | tel. 0431 2 46 01 36. 95 km/59 mi north*

UDHAGAMANDALAM (OOTY)

(150 B2) *(🕮 D10)* ★ **Between 1858 and 1947, to escape from the summer**

heat of the plains, the British Raj withdrew to the cooler climes of the hills.

From there, they even managed to carry on with government business, and thus the so-called *hill stations* such as *Ooty, Munnar, Coonoor* and *Kodaikanal* became very well known in South India. The temperature in the highlands can dip as low as freezing in the winter.

Nestled in a hilly landscape, amongst green tea plantations and forests of pine and eucalyptus, the 'Queen of the Hill Stations', as Ooty (also known as Ootacamund; pop. 384,000) was known, was established in the early 19th century. It extends across broad slopes, its pretty cottages with their flowerbeds bordering the winding roads. On the periphery, however, the more blighted areas resemble Brazilian slums.

The British would spend their time in Ooty playing tennis and golf, riding and socialising. Today it's more about trekking. With its recreational activities, the hill resort is still a very relaxing place to be.

SIGHTSEEING

BOTANICAL GARDEN

With its large areas of lawn, this park-like garden covering 50 acres was created by the British in 1847. It gently rolls across the hillside and has a very English feel. Standing alongside the rare trees, shrubs and flowers, there is also a 20 million-year-old fossilised tree trunk. In the eastern part, on the hill, you can visit the small, Toda tribe village *Munjakal Mund. Daily 7am–7pm | 20 Rs, camera 50 Rs, video 100 Rs*

ST STEPHEN'S CHURCH

This cream-coloured Gothic structure dates back to 1820. It is said that the wood for the construction was taken by British soldiers from Tipu Sultan's Palace in Srirangapatnam and brought to Ooty by elephant. The most distinctive feature of the church is the *Clock Tower. Mysore Rd*

THREAD GARDEN

Fifty women worked on this project for 12 years, using up almost 60 million metres of thread, and ultimately creating an artificial embroidery garden of colourful flowers, plants, lotus ponds, etc. This *four-dimensional embroidery* is a new technique, done without any machines or needles, entirely by hand. *Daily 9am–6pm | 20 Rs, camera 20 Rs, video 30 Rs | on North Lake Rd opposite the boathouse | www.threadgarden.com*

FOOD & DRINK

DHABA EXPRESS

Simple, authentic, cheap, very friendly owners – the speciality is fresh *tandooris* from the wood-fired oven. *Lake View, opposite the boathouse | tel. 0948 6 68 70 74 | Budget*

NAHAR'S SIDE WALK CAFÉ

Italy greets India: in front of guests, pizza chef Saravaman prepares fresh stone-baked pizzas. *52 Charingcross | tel. 0423 2 44 21 73 | www.naharhotels.com | Budget*

SHINKOW

The Chinese restaurant is a tradition. Flavours are slightly adapted to Indian food. *38/83 Commissioners Rd, Upper Bazaar | tel. 0423 2 44 28 11 | Budget–Moderate*

SHOPPING

TIBETAN MARKET

Tibetan refugees sell woolly hats, scarves, gloves and slippers. They also have colourful *tankas,* wall hangings with spiritual symbols. *Opposite the entrance to the Botanical Garden*

SPORTS & ACTIVITIES

BOATS

At the boathouse on the artificially created lake there are all kinds of craft for hire. *Daily 8.30am–7pm | Admission 10 Rs, pedalo and rowing boat 120 Rs (2 seats), 240 Rs (4 seats), 30 min each, motorboat 560 (8 seats), 20 min*

RIDING

It's fun to take a ride along the soft trails outside town. Beginners have a guide to lead the horses. They are usually at places where tourists gather. *From approx. 200 Rs for 30 min*

TREKKING

The *Dodabetta–Snowdon–Ooty Walk* begins at the *Dodabetta Junction.* An easy path winds down through the forest to Ooty. It takes three to four hours and is not tiring. In contrast the two-day tour, *Ooty–Avalanche–Upper Bhavani–Kolaribetta–Emerald–Ooty,* requires a certain level of fitness. It leads from Ooty 24 km/14.9 mi southwest to the Avalanche Dam. After a night spent in the *Forest Department Guest House* *(Wildlife Office | Ooty)* you continue the next day to the Upper Bhavani Lake. A short stretch passes through the *Mukurthi National Park* to Mt Kolaribetta. The climb to the 2625-m/8612-ft ☆ summit is not very taxing and the views are magnificent. On the way back, heading in a northeasterly direction, you will pass the Emerald Lake, from where there are buses back to Ooty. Information: *Office Wildlife Warden, starts on Church Hill Rd | tel. 0423 2 44 59 71*

ENTERTAINMENT

Just how popular the ● movies are in India is demonstrated by the number of cinemas (seven) to be found in Ooty alone. Even if the Bollywood movie isn't dubbed into English, treat yourself to the experience and see how the audience laughs, cries and loves with the actors. Great theatre at the cinema.

WHERE TO STAY

BERRY HILLS RESORT

The whole of Ooty lies at your feet in the lovely new resort below a tea facto-

Not typically Indian, but nice for a change: pedalos on the lake in Ooty

ry. Since it belongs to the same owner, a guided tour is possible of the factory and museum. One disadvantage is the poor condition of the road for about 1 km/0.6 mi. *20 rooms with garden | Stone Hill Post | tel. 0423 2 44 11 26 | www.berryhills.in | Moderate*

FERNHILLS PALACE

Live like a sahib in the colonial period – the former summer residence of the Maharajas of Mysore, with its 19 suites including jacuzzi, conveys precisely this feeling. In the evening, guests meet for an aperitif on the lawn and in the morning are woken up with a cup of tea. *Fernhill Post | tel. 0423 2 44 39 10 | www.welcomheritagehotels.in | Expensive*

GEM PARK HOTEL ⭐

From all 95 rooms of the stylish resort, there are views across the valley. In the evening, from the terrace of the main restaurant you can gaze at the glimmering city lights and the silhouette of the Nilgiri Mountains. In addition, there is a Chinese restaurant, indoor pool, spa, badminton. *Sheddon Rd | tel. 0423 2 44 17 60 | www.gemparkooty.com | Moderate–Expensive*

INFORMATION

TOURIST INFORMATION

Wenlock Rd, next to Tamil Nadu Hotel | tel. 0423 2 44 39 77

WHERE TO GO

DODDABETTA ⭐ (150 B2) (*Ⓜ D10*)

At an altitude of 2638 m/8655 ft this is the highest point in the Nilgiris and its viewing tower offers fantastic views of the surrounding area. Doddabetta means 'high mountain' and it lies some 10 km/6.2 mi east of Ooty, on the border between the Eastern and Western Ghats. You can get to the summit by bus.

MUDUMALAI WILDLIFE SANCTUARY (150 A–B2) (*Ⓜ D–E10*)

Covering an area of 124 mi^2, this large nature reserve forms part of the *Jawaharlal Nehru National Park*. Located 36 km/22.4 mi northwest of Ooty, it was the first wildlife sanctuary in India and it provides a wide variety of landscapes – lowlands, open steppe, swamps and valleys. Elephants, tigers, panthers, red deer and macaque monkeys are all native to the area. Elephant rides and minibus tours are available. From bamboo huts to luxury resorts or tree-houses, everyone will find suitable accommodation in the *Jungle Retreat (Bokkapuram, Masinagudi | tel. 0423 2526469 | www.jungleretreat.com | Budget)*. Away from civilisation, no TV or telephone, but in the national park. *135 Rs | tel. 0423 2 52 62 35*

INSIDER TIP PYKARA (150 B2) (*Ⓜ E10*)

Pykara has for centuries been the homeland of the *Toda*, one of the last remaining mountain tribes of this region. They live in barrel-shaped huts made of grass and bamboo. These buffalo herders are happy to show you their settlements, known as *sholas*.

On the way there, it's worth stopping at the ⭐ boathouse by the dam on the Pykara River to enjoy the beautiful view. *21 km/13.1 mi northeast*

TRIBAL RESEARCH CENTER (150 B2) (*Ⓜ E10*)

The meticulously curated museum offers insights into the culture of the different hill tribes, in particular, the *todas*, still with a population of 1560 in the Nilgiri Mountains. *Mon–Fri 10am–5pm | admission free, small donation welcome. 9 km/5.6 mi south-east*

DISCOVERY TOURS

1 INDIA SOUTH AT A GLANCE

START: 1 Chennai
END: 25 Panaji

24 days
Driving time
(without stops)
49 hours

Distance:
➡ 3000 km/1864 mi

COSTS: approx. 190,500–229,000 Rs (for 2 people incl. hire car with driver, toll charge, meals, overnight accommodation, admissions)

IMPORTANT TIPS: Hire a car with driver for the entire route and insist on good English skills. With an Indian SIM card for all southern states you always have a connection. You can also travel by train: night trains are comfortable, reserve a sleeping compartment!
Book the houseboat beforehand!

Would you like to explore the places that are unique to this region? Then the Discovery Tours are just the thing for you – they include terrific tips for stops worth making, breathtaking places to visit, selected restaurants and fun activities. It's even easier with the Touring App: download the tour with map and route to your smartphone using the QR Code on pages 2/3 or from the website address in the footer below – and you'll never get lost again even when you're offline.

TOURING APP

→ p. 2/3

Immerse yourself in the colourful world of South India and experience the thousand-year-old temples, majestic palaces, lively cities and hip party crowds. And relax meanwhile on the endless dream beaches, in enchanted Backwaters and green tea plantations.

Set off in ❶ **Chennai** → p. 96, where you can visit the white **St Thomas Basilica** which was erected in 1523 on the site of the grave of apostle, St Thomas. In the evening, watch a Bollywood film in the mega complex **Sathyam cinemas**. **Next morning, head south on the State High-**

DAY 1–2

❶ Chennai 🏠 🐾 ⊟

28 km / 17.4 mi

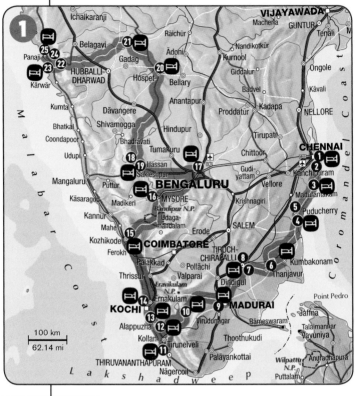

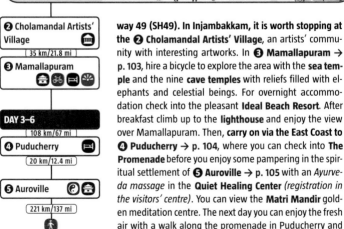

② Cholamandal Artists' Village 🏛
35 km/21.8 mi
③ Mamallapuram 🏛🚲🚌❋

DAY 3–6
108 km/67 mi
④ Puducherry 🛏
20 km/12.4 mi
⑤ Auroville ⓔ🏠
221 km/137 mi
🚶

way 49 (SH49). In Injambakkam, it is worth stopping at the ② **Cholamandal Artists' Village**, an artists' community with interesting artworks. In ③ **Mamallapuram →** p. 103, hire a bicycle to explore the area with the **sea temple** and the nine **cave temples** with reliefs filled with elephants and celestial beings. For overnight accommodation check into the pleasant **Ideal Beach Resort**. After breakfast climb up to the **lighthouse** and enjoy the view over Mamallapuram. Then, **carry on via the East Coast to** ④ **Puducherry →** p. 104, where you can check into **The Promenade** before you enjoy some pampering in the spiritual settlement of ⑤ **Auroville →** p. 105 with an *Ayurveda massage* in the **Quiet Healing Center** *(registration in the visitors' centre)*. You can view the **Matri Mandir** golden meditation centre. The next day you can enjoy the fresh air with a walk along the promenade in Puducherry and

DISCOVERY TOURS

visit **Sri Aurobindo Ashram**. **Then, drive on the NH81 to ⑥ Thanjavur → p. 109**. In the **Paradise Resort**, you can stop over among the rice fields and eat dinner in a tree house. With a good night's sleep, you can explore the **Brihadiswara Temple** before setting off on the **NH83 to ⑦ Tiruchirappalli → p. 110**. Here, **you can climb the 417 steps to Rock Fort** with **Ucchi Pillar Temple**. The reward is a superb panoramic view! Followed by the pool in hotel **Sangam**.

Today, **the NH 38 leads to the temple city of ⑧ Srirangam → p. 110**. Admire the **temple buildings** with their *gopurams* and take a relaxed stroll together with the pilgrims over the **bazaar street**. **Afterwards, head on the NH38 towards ⑨ Madurai → p. 105**. A *tuk-tuk* will transport you across the **bazaar** at the temple. Order a garment from one of the 250 tailors for collection the next morning. From 9pm to 9.30pm you can observe the impressive **Arathi ceremony** with the Shiva statue carried through the temple on a silver litter. Stay overnight in the budget hotel **Chentoor** with a fabulous view from the roof-top terrace. Next morning, you will see South India's greatest marvel – the magnificent **Sri Meenakshi Sundareshwarar Temple** festooned with 33 million figures of gods and demons. Then, you can collect your tailor-made garment; your driver will take **you on the NH85 and 183 into the cool mountains with their tea plantations up to ⑩ Periyar National Park → p. 78**. Here, you can stop for two nights in a grass-covered cottage at **Spice Village**. Next day, with a little luck whether you're on a boat trip, trekking or bamboo rafting, monkeys, elephants and maybe even a tiger will be likely to cross your path. Afterwards, you can visit the **Connemara Tea Factory** and enjoy a guided tour and a cheap cup of tea. **In the morning, the NH183A heads past tea gardens to Kerala's west coast as far as ⑪ Varkala → p. 88**. Relax on the beach and take a dip in the sea, then climb the steps to the top of the **red cliffs** and enjoy the sunset in one of the open-air bars. Next morning, **head along the NH66 and the coast as far as ⑫ Alappuzha → p. 75**. Enjoy the rest of the evening at **Alappuzha Beach** with its street artists. After breakfast, embark on a **houseboat** *(reservations e.g. at info@alleppeyhouseboats.com | tel. 0960 5 98 48 40)* made from bamboo, and recharge your batteries on the enchanted waterways of the **⑬ Backwaters → pp. 75, 92** – including a stopover on board under a starry sky.

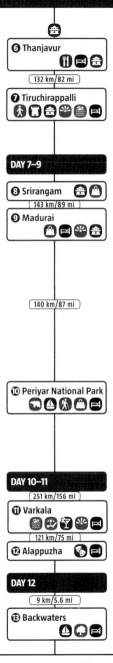

117

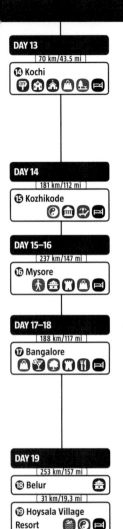

DAY 13

70 km/43.5 mi

⑭ Kochi

DAY 14

181 km/112 mi

⑮ Kozhikode

DAY 15–16

237 km/147 mi

⑯ Mysore

DAY 17–18

188 km/117 mi

⑰ Bangalore

DAY 19

253 km/157 mi

⑱ Belur

31 km/19.3 mi

⑲ Hoysala Village Resort

DAY 20–22

312 km/194 mi

⑳ Hampi

139 km/86 mi

㉑ Badami

Return your houseboat and **head onto the N66 in a northerly direction**. In ⑭ **Kochi** → p. 69 enjoy a stroll through the town and immerse yourself in the bustle of the narrow alleyways in the district of **Fort Kochi**, in its **spice markets**, the **Paradesi Synagogue** and the **cathedral**. In the evening, sit on the sand with a bag of prawns and photograph the **Chinese fishing nets** against the backdrop of the sunset.

Drive to ⑮ **Kozhikode** → **p. 79 on the NH66**. Before you turn in for the night at **Kadavu Resort**, enjoy some oriental treatments in the **beauty salon**. There is a fantastic atmosphere in the evening on the old piers at Kozhikode Beach. **Next day, on Wayanad Rd or the NH766 you will arrive at** ⑯ **Mysore** → **p. 60**, the fairy tale city of the maharajas. Walk up **Chamundi Hill** with Nandi Bull Temple. Book for two nights at the ⓦ **Green Hotel** in the princesses palace. Next morning, admire the magnificent palace of **Amba Villas**, followed by **Devaraja Fruit Market** and the **Sandalwood Factory**, where you can find some souvenirs. The shopping paradise of ⑰ **Bangalore** → p. 46 is **about three-and-a-half hours away on the NH 948**. Is your travel budget still flexible? Silk, jewellery, carpets – along the **MG Road** there is one fabulous shop after another. In the metropolis called Pub City, enjoy a late evening nightcap, e.g. at the **Lock N Load Pub**. Next morning, breathe deeply at the **Lalbagh Botanical Gardens** before you explore the majestic **Bangalore Palace**. In the evening, try **Blue Ginger**, a Vietnamese restaurant in the garden of **Taj West End**.

After a good night's sleep, take the NH75 to ⑱ **Belur** → p. 58. The erotic detail of the images in **Hoysala Temple** is certainly risqué! For overnight accommodation **head south of the pleasant garden area of** ⑲ **Hoysala Village Resort** → **p. 59** in Hassan, where you can easily relax thanks to the pool and spa. **Next morning, take the NH50 to the extensive temple site** ⑳ **Hampi** → **p. 50** – experience the pure magic thanks to its location between bizarre granite rocks along the river. In the evening, chill out in the hammock in the garden of **Shanti Guest House**. Next day you can explore the temple, palaces and triumph chariot on a rental bicycle. After another overnight stay, **on the SH63 head for** ㉑ **Badami** → **p. 54**. Four **cave temples** are hidden in the red sandstone hills. **On the SH34 and NH748, you will reach** the ㉒ **Molem & Bhagvan Mahavir Wildlife Sanctuary** → p. 42 with leopards, elephants and bison. **The entrance is in the western part of the park in Molem. From here, you drive via Colem to Dudhsagar Waterfall**, which plunges 310 m/1017 ft into the depths. The pool invites you to enjoy a refreshing swim. **Via Molem, head back to ㉓ Colva** → p. 38 and the endless beaches of Goa. On the last day, visit ㉔ **Old Goa** → p. 43 with the snow-white church of **Bom Jesus Basilica**. At sunset, treat yourself to a romantic boat trip with dinner and live music on the **Mandovi River** in Goa's capital city ㉕ **Panaji** → p. 40.

DAY 23–24	
208 km/129 mi	
㉒ Molem & Bhagvan Mahavir Wildlife Sanctuary	🐆 🐘 🌊
74 km/46 mi	
㉓ Colva	🏖 🚗
34 km/21.1 mi	
㉔ Old Goa	⛪
13 km/8.1 mi	
㉕ Panaji	⚓ 🍴 🎵 🚗

---

② RIDE BY STEAM TRAIN TO OOTY

START: ❶ Mettupalayam railway station	**2 days**
END: ⓫ Fernhills Palace	Cycling/walking time
Distance:	(without stops)
🔁 78 km/48.5 mi in total	3 ¼ hours

COSTS: approx. 6100 Rs with stopover, admission, board

WHAT TO PACK: food provsions, water, rainwear, hat, sun protection cream

IMPORTANT TIPS: Departure in Mettupalayam daily at 7.10am, arrival at noon in Ooty, advance booking of tickets is essential at *www.indianrail. gov.in*; the ❻ **Botanical Garden** closes between 6pm and 7pm.

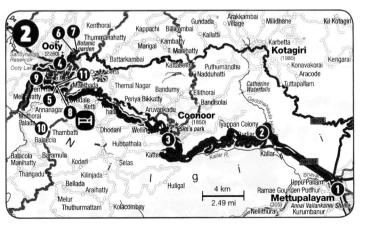

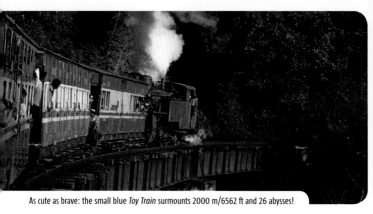

As cute as brave: the small blue *Toy Train* surmounts 2000 m/6562 ft and 26 abysses!

On a narrow metre-gauge track with rack and pinion system, the small *Blue Mountain Train* winds its way through the Niligiri Hills to ascend almost 2000 m/ 6562 ft – the scenery is spectacular with bridges at dizzy heights, long tunnels and deep gorges. From Ooty, the adventure continues on foot and by bicycle to the original sites of the Toda hill tribe.

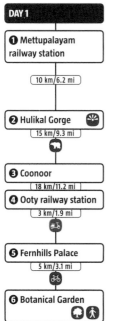

DAY 1

❶ Mettupalayam railway station

[10 km/6.2 mi]

❷ Hulikal Gorge

[15 km/9.3 mi]

❸ Coonoor

[18 km/11.2 mi]

❹ Ooty railway station

[3 km/1.9 mi]

❺ Fernhills Palace

[5 km/3.1 mi]

❻ Botanical Garden

Your tour starts at ❶ **Mettupalayam railway station** *(Ooty Rd | tel. 04254 22 22 85)*, where you board the INSIDER TIP **Blue Mountain Train** *(tickets at the station, reserve beforehand online, Code Mettupalayam (MTP) or Ooty (UAM), train no. 56136 or 56137| 1st class ticket (fabulous view!) single 500 Rs | www.indianrail.gov.in)*. At the very latest, by the time the passengers reach the fourth of twelve station stops along the 46-km/28.6-mi route, they will have got to know how things work aboard the quaint Toy Train. Everybody chats to everyone, shares food and changes seats depending on the view. And that is truly spectacular! In a huge cloud of steam, the locomotive chugs into the hills, travels through 16 tunnels, across 26 bridges and viaducts, which are in part impossibly narrow, and over yawning chasms, such as the one at ❷ **Hulikal Gorge**. Occasionally, adventurous elephants will trot alongside for a short distance. The rack and pinion section finishes in ❸ **Coonoor**, where a diesel locomotive takes over. If you start to smell eucalyptus at some point, you'll know you almost arrived in ❹ **Ooty railway station** → p. 110. Head for ❺ **Fernhills Palace** on the *tuktuk*. At the hotel, check in and hire a bicycle to ride in the afternoon **via the MDR1071 and Commercial Road to the ❻ Botanical Garden. Leave your bicycle here and cross the park to the village of the Todas.** Immersed in the fragrance of exotic flowers and plants, climb up the hill – to about 250 m/820 ft. Immediately below the ridge is the small settlement of the Toda tribe, the **⑦ Toda mund (village)**. The oval *dogle* made from grass and bamboo in a half-barrel shape are making way for new houses. Only the **temple** has retained its original form. The **hand-produced woven items** of the Todas have also remained, such as the woollen shoulder bags in black-white-and red patterns.

After a stopover in the British-colonial atmosphere of **⑧ Fernhills Palace, first cycle on Lake Road along the eastern lake shore.** At the **⑨ boathouse**, hire a boat *(approx. 190 Rs/30 min)* and row across Ooty Lake. Afterwards, continue **by bicycle in the direction of Muthorai Palada. After about 2 km/1.2 mi, the path along the shore meets the MDR 1071.** In Muthorai Palada, finally you reach the **⑩ Tribal Research Center. Shortly before arriving, a forest trail leads uphill. It's best to leave the bicycle at the base and climb the short path on foot.** In the meticulously curated museum, a guide explains the lifestyle of the Todas using examples of tools, clothing and reconstructions of the huts – the Todas are one of India's oldest tribes and they only live in the Niligiri Mountains. Back in **⑪ Fernhills Palace** you can finish your tour in style with a very British afternoon tea.

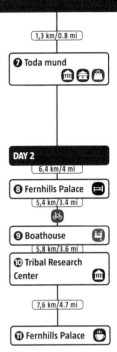

1,3 km/0.8 mi

⑦ Toda mund

DAY 2

6,4 km/4 mi

⑧ Fernhills Palace

5,4 km/3.4 mi

⑨ Boathouse

5,8 km/3.6 mi

⑩ Tribal Research Center

7,6 km/4.7 mi

⑪ Fernhills Palace

---

③ HIKING TO THE TOP OF MEESAPPULIMALA

START: ① Munnar **END: ① Munnar**	**2 days** Walking time (without stops) about 10 hours
Distance: 🕐 approx. 30 km/18.6 mi trekking difficulty level: **moderate**	

COSTS: : approx. 8400 Rs/ 2 persons incl. Sky Cottage, meals, guided tour with a forestry guide

WHAT TO PACK: water, food for the trip, rainwear and sun protection cream (high SPF!), sunglasses, plasters for blisters, walking sticks if required

IMPORTANT TIPS: You should avoid the monsoon season because the trails can then become very slippery. To go trekking, you first have to obtain a permit from the **Kerala Forest Development Cooperation (KFDC)** *(Floriculture Center Madupatty Rd | Munnar | tel. 04865 23 03 32 | www.kfdcecotourism.com)*. Solo travellers must also pay the trekking charges for 2 people. It is compulsory to be accompanied by a forestry guide.

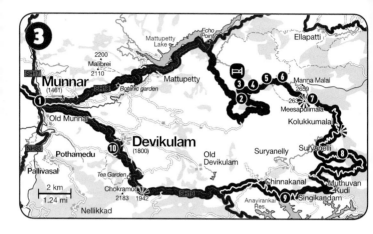

Hiking in the magnificent scenery of Western Ghats is a special experience with the huge variety of flora and fauna. The view from the summit at 2640 m/8661 ft is breathtaking.

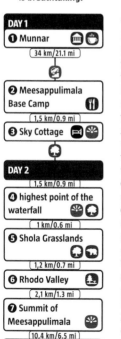

DAY 1

❶ Munnar 🏛️ ☕
┌─ 34 km/21.1 mi ─┐
🚙

❷ Meesappulimala Base Camp 🍴
┌─ 1,5 km/0.9 mi ─┐

❸ Sky Cottage 🏠 ❄️
🌳

DAY 2
┌─ 1,5 km/0.9 mi ─┐

❹ highest point of the waterfall ❄️ 🌳
┌─ 1 km/0.6 mi ─┐

❺ Shola Grasslands 🌳 🐗
┌─ 1,2 km/0.7 mi ─┐

❻ Rhodo Valley 🌿
┌─ 2,1 km/1.3 mi ─┐

❼ Summit of Meesappulimala ❄️
┌─ 10,4 km/6.5 mi ─┐

❽ Papathy Shola 🌿

Your tour begins in **❶ Munnar → p. 77**. To get in the mood, here you will visit the Munnar Tea Museum, where you will learn all the facts about cultivation, production, tea varieties and naturally taste some tea. Then, you set off from the KFDC office by jeep to **❷ Meesappulimala Base Camp**. Here you will eat dinner, breakfast and load up the provisions. A 30-minute trek on foot brings you to the cliff and the isolated location of **❸ INSIDERTIP Sky Cottage** *(2 persons/night approx. 4200 Rs)*, a mountain hut for two people, which has windows on three sides and is opposite a waterfall. The trek starts in the morning with a steep climb past the hut through pine and eucalyptus forests as far as the **❹ highest point of the waterfall**. Afterwards, across vast grasslands there is a steady but moderate climb uphill. The **❺ Shola Grasslands** with their tall ferns and wild orchids are a habitat for deer, bison and giant squirrels. The evergreen rainforest and grassy hills also offer protection for the endangered *Niligiri tahr*, a native species of mountain goat. With their curved horns the brown-coloured *tahrs* look curiously down on the hikers. Numerous tiny streams cross your path. The water is crystal clear and ice cold. After about 3 hours you will reach the **❻ Rhodo Valley** at an altitude of 2325 m/7628 ft and surrounded by a grove of wild rhododendrons. After a rest, the ascent begins, first on a slope, then continuing along partly hollowed out trails where you can only go forward in single file, over-all for 8 km/5 mi, and uphill. Only the last third of the trail becomes steeper and exhausting. It is well worth the effort – after two hours, you have reached the ❼ **Summit of Meesappulimala** at 2640 m/8661 ft. The 360-degree panorama of the tea plantations deep below, the blue glimmering lakes and with good visibility the view of the summits of the Kodaikanal is simply breathtaking! On the way back, you pass ❽ **Papathy Shola** – the butterfly forest. Especially in October/ November, thousands of brightly coloured butterflies float about in all imaginable colours and patterns through the sparse mixed forest. The descent contin-

Munnar: tea cannot taste better than directly from the plantation.

ues past ❾ **Anaerangal Lake**. With a little luck in the evening you can see thirsty elephants quench their thirst in the lake. By late afternoon, you have arrived in the valley. Now you can enjoy another cup of tea at one of the ❿ **stalls** on the trail back to ❶ **Munnar**; the strong and fragrant taste – fresh from the plantation – is unique.

13,3 km/8.3 mi
❾ Anaerangal Lake
16 km/9.9 mi
❿ stalls
7 km/4.4 mi
❶ Munnar

④ BICYCLE TOUR TO THE MANDOVI ISLANDS

START: ❶ Santa Cruz	1 day
END: ❶ Santa Cruz	Cycling time
Distance:	(without stops)
🕐 43 km/26.7 mi	3 hours

COSTS: approx. 3960 Rs incl. bicycle hire, admission to the bird park, bird guide, canoe, lunch, Fenni bar
WHAT TO PACK: binoculars, rainwear and sun protection (high SPF!), water

IMPORTANT TIPS: Book the bicycles in advance! On the major streets of the mainland there are no separate cycling routes – pay attention to the road-traffic. On the islands, you can easily travel by bicycle.

Near Panaji, multiple channels of the Mandovi River have created a natural network of fluvial arteries. At the centre lie the islands of Divar and Chorao with small villages, mangrove forests and green rice fields, with rare birds, rustic Fenni bars and enchanted temples – ideal for INSIDER TIP ▶ a relaxed cycling tour.

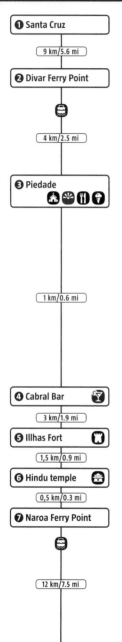

1 Santa Cruz

9 km/5.6 mi

2 Divar Ferry Point

4 km/2.5 mi

3 Piedade

1 km/0.6 mi

4 Cabral Bar

3 km/1.9 mi

5 Illhas Fort

1,5 km/0.9 mi

6 Hindu temple

0,5 km/0.3 mi

7 Naroa Ferry Point

12 km/7.5 mi

09:00am The tour begins in **1** **Santa Cruz**, where Bianca Dias from **Offtrail Adventures** *(H. No. 112 Bandh., Nx | tel. 099756 5 09 07 | www.offtrail.in)* offers good bicycles for hire. Afterwards, **head on the road from Panaji to Belgaum as far as the 2 Divar Ferry Point** *(daily 6am–midnight every 15 min | free of charge for cyclists/pedestrians)* **in Ribandar.** The journey to **Divar Island** takes five minutes. **Head across the island in the direction of Piedade; on the right-hand side on the opposite side of the river you will pass all the churches of Old Goa.** The route continues through rice fields, only now some isolate houses appear. **You must take another two right turns** to reach **3 Piedade**, the heart of the 5.8 mi² island. From a distance, you will already notice on a small hill the white **Church of Our Lady of Compassion** from the early 16th century. From here you can enjoy the superb view into the distance of the idyllic rural landscape, the meandering Mandovi River and as far as Old Goa. In Piedade, you will find peaceful Goan rural life with charming houses in Portuguese style, with column verandas and mango trees in the gardens.

12:30pm For lunch, the pleasant **Café Harmalkar** serves reasonably priced snacks, such as *samosas* with *lassi*. For dessert, cyclists treat themselves to an ice cream from the bakery **Marita & Co**. **A bigger street then leads in the direction of the Naroa Ferry Point, which is about 3.5 km/2.2 mi away.** On the way, you should definitely taste the Fenni schnapps which is made from Cashew nuts, e.g. at **4 Cabral Bar**, which is mainly frequented by farmers and fishermen. **Turn off at the main crossroads about 200 m/656 ft in a south-easterly direction.** At Naroa, stop for a while at the 17th-century **5 Illhas Fort**, or rather what remains. On the way to the ferry in a palm grove there is a small **6 Hindu temple** – one of the many temples spread across the island.

03:00pm In the afternoon at the **7 Naroa Ferry Point** at Divra's north-eastern point take the ferry across the river to Narwe district. To the sound of peacock calls, **take a left turn after 1 km/0.6 mi and cycle on the right-hand side along the rail tracks and then cross over the narrow river on the bridge.** Now you are on the peninsula of **Chorao Island**. **The route carries on through green fields, in part lined with palm trees, as far as the western tip of Chorao. About 50 m/164 ft**

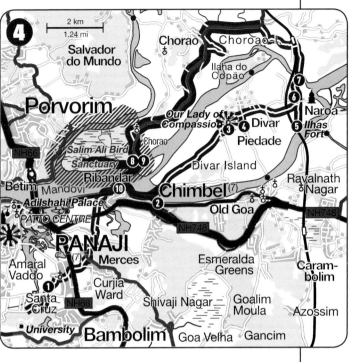

alongside **Chorao Ferry Point** is the entrance to the 440-acre **❽ Dr Salim Ali' Bird Sanctuary** *(daily 6am–6pm | admission 50 Rs, camera 30 Rs)*, named after India's most famous ornithologist. The area is covered with low mangroves and is accessible thanks to paved footpaths. Bridges lead to observation posts far into the water for swamp crocodiles, otters, crabs and South sea fish. Some fishermen also hire out canoes with which you can complete a **Paddle tour** *(1.5 hour, 700 Rs)* at high tide. The best view is from a **viewpoint** in the middle of the mangroves. Discover some of about 200 bird species through the binoculars – can you make out the flash of ice blue of the Kingfisher, eagles, cormorants catching fish, storks, sandpipers or curlews? Or the flying fox which hangs upside down in the branches during the daytime? Afterwards, the ferry takes you to **❾ Chorao Ferry Point** *(every 15 min until midnight)* and to **❿ Ribandar** to the mainland, where you can enjoy the easy bicycle ride back to **❶ Santa Cruz**.

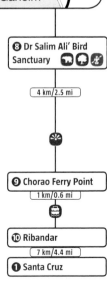

❽ Dr Salim Ali' Bird Sanctuary

4 km/2.5 mi

❾ Chorao Ferry Point

1 km/0.6 mi

❿ Ribandar

7 km/4.4 mi

❶ Santa Cruz

SPORTS & ACTIVITIES

The mountains and sea offer active holidaymakers so many opportunities in India that are incredibly diverse and exciting. Those looking for total relaxation and recuperation will find – in addition to Ayurveda spa offers – a wide selection of wellness programmes that are entirely sustainable thanks to the climate and they are also much more reasonably priced.

BOLLYWOOD DANCING

Bollywood films with their amazing dance routines are not only popular in South India. Movie choreographer Arun Kumar teaches novices in Bengaluru *(Forum Value Mall, No. 62, 2nd floor, Whitefield Main Rd | Whitefield near* Bengaluru | tel. 095 91 75 70 29) the **INSIDER TIP** Bollywood dance moves. The famous choreographer Shiamak Davar (Slumdog Millionaire) combines Bollywood with jazz dance *(Richmond Tower, No. 109, 1st floor, 12, Richmond Rd | Bengaluru | tel. 080 41 31 76 61 | www.shiamak.com).*

CRICKET

Nowhere is more passionate about cricket than India. Almost the entire nation defines itself through this sport, which the British introduced to the subcontinent around 1900. Visit one of the large stadiums to experience the special atmosphere of a game at first-hand. *The M. A. Chidambaram Stadium*

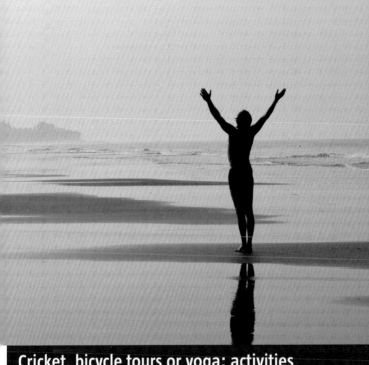

Cricket, bicycle tours or yoga: activities for outdoor fans, stressed visitors and advocates of exercises for mind and body

Chennai (Wallajah Rd | tel. 044 28 58 88 89 | 50,000 spectators) occupies a special place in cricketing history: in 1962 it was the venue for the country's first win over England. The *M. Chinnaswamy Stadium Bangalore (Cubbon Rd/Queens Rd | tel. 080 40 15 40 15)* can accommodate up to 55,000 spectators. There are numerous cricket teams in Goa, and they all play at the *Rajandra Prasad Stadium (Free admission, you only pay at international matches | Quepem Rd | tel. 0832 2 73 14 95)*.

DIVING & WATERSPORTS

South India's best dive sites are located in the north of Karnataka, off *Pigeon Island* opposite Bhatkal. An impressive underwater world opens up among the reefs and numerous wrecks. In Goa most dive boats head for *San Jorge Island* or *Grande Island*. Wrecks of Spanish and Portuguese galleons lie on the seabed, as well as a ship from World War II. Diving centres: *Goa Beach Sports Academy | Cobra Vaddo, Calangute |*

tel. 098 22 12 21 71 | goabeachsportacad
emy.com; Goa Diving | Bimtan, Bogmalo
Beach, Chiconia | tel. 090 49 44 26 47 |
www.goadiving.com. The *Goa Beach
Sports Academy* also teaches windsurfing.
The PADI Diving Centre *Temple Adven-
tures (tel. 099 40 21 94 49 | www.tem
pleadventures.com)* also offers a diving
tour to the diving sites off Puducherry.
In many places in South India, *Sport-
sphere (tel. 088 84 47 72 50 | www.
sportsphere.in)* from Bangalore offers
the whole range of water sports such as
surfing, sailing, kitesurfing, wakeboard-
ing, diving, snorkelling and river rafting.

GOLF

Many old clubhouses still have lots of
colonial charm, such as the *Bangalore
Golf Club* dating from 1876 *(18-hole |
2 Sankey Rd, High Grounds | tel. 080 41
31 76 61, -2, -3)* or the *Madras Gymkhana
Club* in Chennai *(18-hole | Anna Salai | tel.
044 25 36 81 68 | www.madrasgymkhana.
com)*. The *Ootacamund Gymkhana Club
(18-hole | Ekaly Rd | tel. 0423 2 44 22 54 |
www.ootygolfclub.org)* dates from 1896;
its course lies on steep terrain at an altitude of 2300 m/7546 ft.

TREKKING

The Western Ghats, which include the
Nilgiri Mountains, are a great place for
trekking. Rising to a maximum altitude
of approx. 2600 m/8530 ft, these mountains are easily accessible for every hiker.
For trails that are hard to follow and lead
through jungle areas, trekkers should ac-
quire a guide from the respective Forest
Department. To traverse protected areas
you will also need to have a permit. Nil-
giri Mountains: *District Forest Officer | Nil-
giris North Division | Mount Stuart Hill |
Ooty | tel. 0423 2 44 39 68;* Munnar:

*Forest Information Centre | tel. 04865
23 15 87;* Kumily: *District Tourist Informa-
tion Office | next to the private Bus Stand |
tel. 04869 22 26 20.* The best times for
trekking are April to June and September
to December.

Organised walks are operated by the
*District Tourism Promotion Council
(DTPC) Idukki, Kochi-Dhanushkodi Rd,
Moolakadai, Munnar | tel. 04856 23 15 16.*
Further information from *Muddy Boots,*
experts in trekking and mountain-biking
tours, as well as contact point for general
questions on trekking in South India *(in
England – Pradeep Murthy – tel. 0044
78 26 72 87 07, in India 095 44 20 12 49 |
www.muddyboots.in).*

Special tours are offered for the rustic
Periyar Tiger Reserve. Here, you can trek
with INSIDER TIP former smugglers and
poachers – it doesn't get more authentic
than that! As part of the ⊕ eco-develop-
ment project for the social integration of
the hill tribes these tough guys were
retrained as nature guides and now
accompany hiking groups on combined
bamboo rafting and trekking tours in the
mountains of Western Ghats. Now, the
guns belonging to the guides only serve
as protection for the trekking group –
from tigers, leopards, wild elephants and
bears. The men belong to three mountain tribes around Thekkady that have
managed to preserve their identity to the
present day. It isn't just the five guides in
the ten-person group (maximum number of members), plus the armed securi-
ty guard, that make this trek so different;
just walking in the jungle itself, through
the densest part of the Periyar National
Park, is something very special.

Along the route, the guides tell stories
about their lives as smugglers and
poachers which was more lucrative, but
also ten times more dangerous. However, they regain some of that lost ex-

citement with their night-time smuggler hunting forays.

Information in Thekkady: *Periyar Tiger Reserve Organisation | Lake Rd | tel. 04869 22 20 27* or *Forest Information and Reservation Centre | Ambady Junction, Lake Rd | tel. 04869 32 20 28 |* both daily

There are two reputable centres located in Bengaluru: Jindal Nature Cure *Institute (Jindal PG College | Mud Track Rd, Maruti Layout, Aanchepalya Village | tel. 080 23 71 77 77 | www.jindalnature cure.in* and *Svyasa Yoga University (19 Eknath Bhavan, Gavipuram Circle, K. G.*

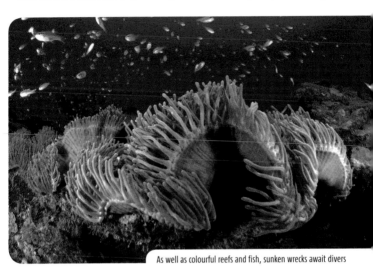

As well as colourful reefs and fish, sunken wrecks await divers

6am–7pm or at the *Spice Village Hotel | Kumily Rd | tel. 04869 22 45 14 | www. cghearth.com. Periyar National Park* opening times 6am–5pm | admission 300 Rs | whole-day trekking with bamboo rafting 2000 Rs, with one night in the tent camp 5000 Rs, 2 nights 7000 Rs

YOGA

Many hotels and resorts offer yoga classes. The morning group sessions are mostly free. There's a big choice of yoga centres and courses in **INSIDER TIP** *Auroville (tel. 0413 2 62 27 04 | www.auroville. org).* The inexpensive accommodation there may enable visitors to attend courses for longer.

Nagar | tel. 080 26 60 86 45 | svyasa. edu.in. At the *Ashtanga Yoga Research Institute (235 8th Cross, Gokulam | tel. 098 80 18 55 00 | www.kpjayi.org)* in Mysore they teach rapid breathing exercises, while at the *Krishnamacharya Yoga Mandiram (31 4th Cross St, R K Nagar | tel. 044 24 93 79 98 | www.kym. org)* in Chennai they do viniyoga, a gentler version of yoga. Also in Chennai, in the early morning from 6–8am you can join in ● free yoga classes at a total of 26 public open spaces, including Panagal Park and Marina Beach. With the health of his fellow citizens at heart, Chennai's former mayor had the necessary stages built and appointed yoga instructors.

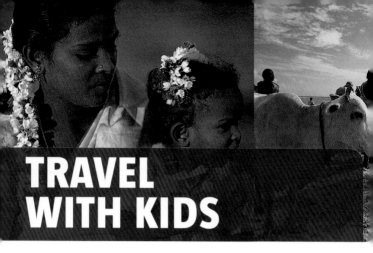

TRAVEL WITH KIDS

What sounds like an advertising slogan for the tourism sector is, in fact, the case: Indians love children. And that isn't just a good thing for the kids but also for the grown-ups, as children often help everyone make friends.

South India is tremendously exciting territory for the young. The exotic animals, the giant sand pit known as the beach, and all the friendly people, who never complain when things get a bit noisy and boisterous. But there are a few things you should consider if you're travelling with children in South India. One is of course the strong tropical sun, which will necessitate a sun hat and using sunscreen with a very high protection factor. Then there is the hot and spicy food, which youngsters probably won't be used to; so, you should always ask for milder dishes for the kids. And finally there are all those dogs – they might look nice and playful, but be careful, they can also bite!

GAME PARKS

South India has lots of game parks, notably in the state of Karnataka. The *Bandipur National Park* (150 B1–2) (*ᗝ D–E10*) in the borderlands of Kerala, Karnataka and Tamil Nadu, for example, is a designated tiger reserve. Near Coorg in Karnataka, the *Dubare Elephant Camp* (147 F5) (*ᗝ D9*) is home to 150 elephants. However, most of the region's wild Asian elephants live in the *Nagarhole National Park* (148 A5) (*ᗝ D9*). Along with tigers and leopards, the pachyderms are also found in the *Bhadra Tiger Reserve* (147 F3) (*ᗝ C–D8*). The *Mudumalai Wildlife Sanctuary* (150 A–B2) (*ᗝ D–E10*) covers an area of 124 mi² and contains a large variety of animals, including elephants, panthers, bears, monkeys. You can find detailed information about animals and tours at *www.indianwildlifeportal.com, www.wild-india.com, www.indiawildliferesorts.com* and *www.indian-wildlife.com*.

GOA

ANCESTRAL GOA (144 A5) (*ᗝ B6*)
At the so-called *Big Foot Village* in Loutolim (9 km/5.6 mi from Margao, 45 km/28 mi from Calangute), colourful, naive figures and props give children a fun introduction to the roots of Goan culture. *Daily 9am–6pm | admission adults 50 Rs, children from 3–10 years 25 Rs, camera 20 Rs | ancestralgoa.com*

Indians love children: youngsters will find plenty of exciting things to do, from riding on an elephant to visiting a crocodile farm

SPLASH DOWN WATERPARK
(144 A5) (*Ⓜ B6*)

Wonderfully refreshing, and lots of fun for all age groups. With five pools, a variety of water slides which demand more or less courage. Attractive for older age groups: Aqua Dance – disco in the rain – pretty cool. *Daily 10.30am–6pm | Admission adults 400 Rs, children 360 Rs | Calangute-Anjuna Main Rd, Padre Agnel Vaddo, Gauvaddi | at the Double Tree Hilton Hotel, Bardez*

KERALA

WONDERLA KOCHI (150 A4) (*Ⓜ D11)*)

A large theme park with water slides, rides, musical fountains and many other attractions. It has a sister company in Bangalore. *Mon–Fri 11am–6pm, Sat/Sun 11am–7pm | admission adults from 750 Rs, children (90–140 cm/35.5–55 in) from 600 Rs | Pallikara near Kakkanad, 14 km/8.7 mi northeast of Kochi | www.wonderla.com*

KARNATAKA

PILIKULA BIOLOGICAL PARK
(147 E4) (*Ⓜ C9*)

Your children can go riding on elephants at the large park in Pilikula near Mangalore. There are also lots of other animals to look at, as well as a funfair with giant slide, a water park and boating lake. *Tue–Sun 9.30am–5.30pm | admission from 12 years and over 50 Rs, under 12 20 Rs, photo 30 Rs, video 125 Rs | Moodushedde, Vamanjoor | www.pilikula.com*

TAMIL NADU

MADRAS CROCODILE BANK
(149 F4) (*Ⓜ H9*)

About 40 km/24.9 mi south of Chennai, various kinds of Indian crocodiles and alligators are kept in open pools. *Tue–Sun 8.30am–5.30pm | admission adults 40 Rs, children up to 10 years 20 Rs, camera 20 Rs, video 100 Rs | on the coast road | www.madrascrocodilebank.org*

FESTIVALS & EVENTS

Most religious holidays are calculated according to the lunar calendar and are therefore movable.

6 JANUARY
The festival of *Epiphany* is celebrated in Goa – principally in Cansaulim, Chandor and Reis Magos.

END FEBRUARY/BEGINNING MARCH
★ *Shivaratri* or *Mahashivaratri*: the Night of Shiva is the holiest night for Hindus and is spent at the temple.

MARCH
The Indian *Holi Festival* is celebrated especially colourfully in Goa, where it is known as the *Shigmo Festival*. Temple festivals, parades, processions.

AUGUST
Janmashtami: Krishna's Birthday, involving midnight festivals at the Hindu temples.

SEPTEMBER/OCTOBER
★ *Dussehra*: India's best-known festival is celebrated in different ways in different places. It celebrates the victory of the gods Rama and Durga over the demons.

In the South it is called *Navaratri*. In Tamil Nadu and Karnataka the festivities go on for nine nights; in Mysore, it lasts for ten days with music festivals in the illuminated palace. On the tenth day an impressive procession of elephants leads to the Maharaja's palace.

NOVEMBER/DECEMBER
INSIDER TIP ▶ *Divali* – the Festival of Light: everywhere fireworks illuminate the sky and small oil lamps are lit in honour of Lakshmi, the goddess of wealth and prosperity.

FESTIVALS

At the *Float Festival* in Madurai, temple deities are paraded around the sacred Mariamman Teppakolam Lake on a brightly decorated float.
Pongal is the name given to the harvest festival, which takes place during the religious celebrations of *Makar Sankranti*. Cows are decorated with balloons and garlands, and their horns colourfully painted before they are led through the streets to musical accompaniment.

FEBRUARY
This *Food & Cultural Festival* which lasts between three to five days is held alter-

Elephants on parade, snake boat races, festivals of light – South Indian celebrations are always full of pomp and splendour

nately in Panaji and Margao; it includes cooking contests, stalls selling typical food, and lots of music and dance.

FEBRUARY/MARCH
Natyanjali Dance Festival at the Nataraja Temple in Chidambaram. Famous dancers from all over India come to this five-day festival in honour of Shiva as Nataraja, the 'Lord of Dance'; now, celebrations are held not only here but also at other temples in Tamil Nadu.

Carnival or *Mardi Gras* is celebrated all over Goa. On the first day, *Fat Saturday*, 'King Momo' leads a parade of colourfully-dressed through the streets.

APRIL/MAY
During the eight-day *Pooram Festival* (summer harvest festival) at Thrissur in Kerala, various temples compete to see who has the most beautiful parade of finely decorated elephants. There are also Kathakali performances and firework displays.

AUGUST/SEPTEMBER
Kerala's snake boat races are linked with the *Onam,* the harvest festival. Every boat carries 25 singers and up to 125 towers. The most famous regatta is the *Nehru Trophy* on Punnamada Lake in Alappuzha on the 2nd Sunday in August.

MID-DECEMBER–MID-JANUARY
At the ● *Chennai Music and Dance Festival* artists from all over India play classical music and perform traditional dances on squares, at temples and in heritage bungalows. More than 2000 people take part in over 300 concerts.

PUBLIC HOLIDAYS

1 Jan	New Year's Day
26 Jan	Republic Day
1 May	Labour Day
15 Aug	Independence Day
2 Oct	Gandhi's Birthday
25 Dec	Christmas

LINKS, BLOGS, APPS & MORE

www.mapsofindia.com One of the most valuable links for South India travellers. Here you will find detailed maps and train and flight connections, also for the rest of India

www.discoverbangalore.com Everything about India's Silicon Valley – Bangalore. This site has continuously updated information and tips on all kinds of themes related to the city: events, restaurants, sights and much more

www.wwfindia.org and www.traffic.org Protecting wildlife means thinking about it before you buy a souvenir in South India. Especially if they're products made of crocodile skin, ivory, coral, or certain protected plants. WWF and Traffic India explain all the issues on their websites

www.goablog.org Goa's top beaches, the best parties, the most effective yoga courses, its history, culture and politics, upcoming events – bloggers from around the world share interesting information on a large range of themes relating to India's smallest state

Indianbloggers.org Here, the best Indian blogs are listed on all kinds of subjects such as spirituality, literature, Bollywood actors, wildlife, journalists, travel, lifestyle, food and much more

templenet.com/karnataka.html Provides information on the most important temples in Karnataka. Every description includes helpful links

Regardless of whether you are still preparing your trip or already in South India: these addresses will provide you with more information, videos and networks to make your holiday even more enjoyable.

VIDEOS & MUSIC

short.travel/inds2 A collection of short clips on Kerala's Backwater with exceptional underwater and landscape photos. Inspires you to take a trip on a houseboat

short.travel/inds3 Atmospheric pictures of a journey to the most beautiful temples of South India

short.travel/inds4 A tour of all South India in just nine minutes – loud, condensed and vibrant – a kaleidoscope of thousands of impressions, compiled during the cameraman's two-month trip through the southern subcontinent

short.travel/inds6 The popular magazine Timeout has compiled the ten best Bollywood dance scenes – each with a short video

APPS

Indian Rail Info This free app provides arrival and departure information for trains, shows available seats/sleepers, ticket prices and much more

www.indianrailapp.com is the fastest website for checking free seats

AccuWeather Most weather Apps are not suitable in India where the most reliable one is the international App AccuWeather – as the name already suggests with accurate local forecasts

NGpay This App enables you to book tickets for trains on Indian Rail and all major Indian bus routes as well as flight tickets of various airlines while you are on the move

TRAVEL TIPS

ARRIVAL

✈ Most visitors to South India arrive by plane. Condor and Thomson Flights fly direct to Goa from London. Qatar Airways also operates flights from London via Doha. British Airways go to Bangalore from London in approx. 10 hrs. Serving Goa from the USA are American Airlines, Air India, Qatar Airways and US Airways. Bangalore is also served by Emirates, Lufthansa, KLM, Etihad and Air France.

BANKS & EXCHANGE

Opening times: Mon–Fri 10am–2pm, Sat 10am–noon. At many cashpoints you can withdraw rupees with your debit/credit card. Bureaux de change and even bank counters at the airports offer better changing rates than the banks. Tip: just change a small amount of money at the airport and then look for a bureau de change at your destination. Many large shops and hotels accept the usual credit cards.

RESPONSIBLE TRAVEL

It doesn't take a lot to be environmentally friendly whilst travelling. Don't just think about your carbon footprint whilst flying to and from your holiday destination but also about how you can protect nature and culture abroad. As a tourist it is especially important to respect nature, look out for local products, cycle instead of driving, save water and much more. If you would like to find out more about eco-tourism please visit: *www.ecotourism.org*

CAR HIRE WITH DRIVER

It is more comfortable and safer to be chauffeured around, rather than taking public transport. Hiring a car without a driver is not recommended due to the chaotic traffic, not to mention the fact that the difference in price is very small. Always make sure that the driver speaks good English. Almost all travel agencies in South India arrange *chauffeured cars.* Tours can also be booked from home, with accommodation. Try *India Invites* in Goa *(tel. 0091 832 2 71 57 81 | www.india invites.com)*, or *Inter-Car* in Kerala *(tel. 0091 471 2 33 04 17 | www.ariestravel.net).*

CLIMATE, WHEN TO GO

Apart from the highlands, a hot, tropical climate prevails in South India. The period from November to March is the coolest and therefore the best time to travel for westerners used to cooler climes. It is pleasantly warm mornings and evenings, and the days are dry and sunny. The monsoon rains come to southwest India from April to July, to the southeast from October to November.

CONSULATES & EMBASSIES

BRITISH DEPUTY HIGH COMMISSION
Bangalore | Prestige Takt, 23 Kasturba Cross Road | Bangalore 560001, South India | tel. +91 80 2210 0200 | www.gov. uk/world/organisations/british-deputy-high-commission-bangalore

BRITISH DEPUTY HIGH COMMISSION
Chennai | 20 Anderson Road | Chennai 600 006 | tel. +91 44 421 921 51 | Email: web.newdelhi@fco.gov.uk

From arrival to weather

Holiday from start to finish: useful addresses and information for your trip to India

UK CONSULATE
Goa | 303–304 Casa del Sol, opposite Marriott Hotel | Miramar, Panaji 403 001 | tel. +91 832 6636 777 | Email: consular.goa@fco.gov.uk

US CONSULATE GENERAL
Chennai | Gemini Circle | Chennai 600 006 | tel. +91 44 2857 4000 | in.usembassy.gov/embassy-consulates/chennai/

CURRENCY

The local currency is the Indian rupee (INR, unofficially Rs). One rupee is equal to 100 paise. There are coins in denominations of 10, 25 and 50 paise and 1, 2 and 5 rupees. Notes are in denominations of 1, 2, 5, 10, 20, 50, 100, 500 and 1000 rupees.

CUSTOMS

Currency exceeding the value of 5000 US$/ 3860 £ must be declared on arrival. Any expensive items (e.g. video cameras) should also be declared. The import and export of Indian currency is prohibited. The following quantities may be imported in the EU (per person aged 18 or above): 200 cigarettes, 50 cigars or 250 g tobacco, 1 l alcohol above and 2 l alcohol up to 22 vol.%, 500 g coffee, other goods such as tea, perfume and gifts up to 390 £/574 US$.

DENTAL TREATMENT

Want to see a dentist in India? It's not such an absurd idea. The surgeries are modern, most dentists have trained in England or the USA and can carry out professional root canal treatments, perform implants, crowns and whitening. The advantage:

costs are between one third and half of those in the west, there are no waiting lists, and some resorts, such as *Poovar Island Resort (tel. 0471 2 21 20 68 | www.poovarislandresort.com)* in Kerala, work together with dental surgeries. That means that after the pain comes the relaxation – a kind of reward in the form of Ayurveda or wellness treatments. Most dentists for tourists are located in Goa, followed by Kerala.

CURRENCY CONVERTER

£	INR	INR	£
1	83	10	0.12
3	249	30	0.36
5	415	50	0.60
13	1079	130	1.56
40	3320	400	4.80
75	6225	750	9
120	9960	1200	14.40
250	20,75	5000	60
500	41,50	15,000	180

$	INR	INR	$
1	64	10	0.16
3	192	30	0.48
5	320	50	0.80
13	832	130	2.08
40	2560	400	6.40
75	4800	750	12
120	7680	1200	19.20
250	16,000	5000	80
500	32,000	15,000	240

For current exchange rates see www.xe.com

ELECTRICITY

The usual power supply is 220 volt AC with a frequency of 50 Hz. There are different plug sockets in India, so bring along a variety of adaptors – or buy on the spot.

BUDGETING

Rickshaw	1.15 £/1.45 US$ per km; minimum of 1.30 £/1.70 US$
Tea	0.14 £/0.19 US$ per cup
Sun lounger	from 1.75 £/2.25 US$ with parasol rent
Dosa	from 0.80 £/1 US$ for one portion, stuffed
Massage	from 11.50–17.50 £/ 14.50–22.50 US$ Ayurvedic
Cinema	from 2.10 £/2.70 US$ for one ticket

GOING OUT

Many nightclubs will only admit couples. If you're single it's best to find out beforehand. Dance bars in luxury hotels are often only open to guests. Each state has different closing times for nightclubs and bars, which often change. *Pub City* in Bangalore has the coolest and most stylish discos. In Goa, meanwhile, romantic beach parties are held on the beaches in the north and silent parties with headphones on the beach in Palolem.

HEALTH

No vaccinations are necessary for visitors arriving from the UK or USA. To be on the safe side, however, you can be vaccinated against typhoid and hepatitis. A malaria prophylaxis is recommended in any event. Make sure you obtain the requisite travel insurance including cover for repatriation. In case of accident or illness in India either have your hotel call their contracted doctor or go straight to a private clinic which will provide a better standard of hygiene and medical care than the public hospitals. Costs have to be paid up front – make sure you have enough money to hand.

IMMIGRATION

Tourist visas (basic fee approx. 7250 Rs) are issued for a period of 12 months, and multiple visits are possible with a *multiple entry visa*. Visas are issued by the respective departments of the Indian High Commission, Embassy or consulates.

HIGH COMMISSION IN LONDON:
India House | Aldwych, London WC2B 4NA | UK | tel. +44 20 8629 5950 | www. hcilondon.in

EMBASSY IN WASHINGTON, D.C.:
2107 Massachusetts Avenue NW | Washington, D.C., 20008 | USA | tel. +1 202 9397 000 | www.indianembassy.org

Now, tourists can also apply for an e-visa upon arrival (ETV) at *indianvisaonline. gov.in/evisa*. This is possible at the earliest 120 days, and at the latest 4 days before arriving in India. The e-visa is valid for up to 60 days and costs 50 US$.

INFORMATION

INDIAN TOURIST OFFICE
26–28 Hammersmith Grove | London W6 7BA | tel. 0207 43 73 677 | www.incredi bleindia.org

1270 6th Ave #303 | New York, 10020 | tel. 0212 586-4901 | www.tourism.gov.in

INLAND TRAVEL

Even the remotest places in South India

are accessible by public transport. The dense transport network of rail, bus and air connections works well and is inexpensive. For long distances, apart from taking a plane, the train is the best option, as trains are more reliable than buses, which often can't keep to their timetables because of traffic congestion. For short distances, it's worth taking the bus for its affordable prices. Pensioners get big reductions for bus and train travel. Bus tickets can now also be purchased online at *www.redbus.in*.

The brochure 'Trains at a Glance', available from station kiosks, is very useful. Timetables, prices and available places in sleeper carriages can be found online at *www.indianrail.gov.in* and *www.irctc.com*. There are different counters for 1st, 2nd and 3rd class tickets, and often for tourists as well as women *(Ladies Ticket Office)*. Do buy your ticket before reserving your seat. It is almost impossible to book over the phone. But even when the train looks completely booked up, the so-called VIP tickets will usually be still available for a surcharge. It's necessary to make a reservation for night trains with sleeping compartments or carriages. Getting an *Indrail Pass* is only worth it in order to avoid having to stand in the queues at the ticket counters. Otherwise single tickets will end up a bit cheaper.

The whole country is served by a well-developed bus network. Most of the routes are covered by state-run buses, which are often hot and full. Air-conditioned buses, often Volvos, are more expensive but much more comfortable for long journeys. The categories are *ordinary* (hard seats, no air-conditioning), *deluxe* or *luxury*. Buses should at least have a fan. You can get tickets from the counters at

the bus stations and, with some private bus companies, also on board.

The domestic airline market is in a constant state of flux. The former state-run Indian Airlines has now merged with Air India. New private airlines are being created while others are being closed down. At the present time there are about 10 domestic airlines operating in India, including Air India, GoAir, Indigo, Spicejet, Jet Airways.

INTERNET CAFÉS & WI-FI

Everywhere in India you'll find a internet café. However, the connections are sometimes painfully slow. Most hotels have Wi-Fi hotspots, and you can surf in cafés and restaurants in the cities and resorts.

PERSONAL SAFETY

If women travelling alone observe a few simple rules, India is a safe destination. Of course, they should avoid wearing provocative clothing and not to go on walks after dark. The author herself has travelled for many years in India, often on her own. She avoids asking men the way or the time of day because that can be misunderstood, or she wears a scarf over her face as an unspoken signal of Indian women who don't wish to be spoken to. Wearing a Salvar Kameez, a long top over slim-leg trousers, she doesn't look like a newcomer. Please study the official travel advice before you set off.

PHONE & MOBILE PHONE

The ISD (International Subscriber Dialing) telephone shops are slowly disappearing – previously, even in the smallest villages you could still make telephone calls abroad. Many Internet shops are still open and almost every hotel has WiFi. Code from India to the UK: *0044*, to the USA *001*. From abroad, you can call India using the code *0091*. In all cases, omit the zero from the local code. International calls are reasonable. If you have a mobile you should use an Indian pay-as-you-go SIM card. With that you can make calls within India and back home cheaper than going through your own provider. Important: take along a copy of your passport and two passport photos. Emergency services: police *tel. 100*, fire service *tel. 101*, ambulance: *tel. 102* and *108* in Tamil Nadu

POST

It's best to hand in your letters and post-cards at hotels or post offices, rather than using a post box. Postcards, too, should be marked 'Airmail'. Sending a postcard from India to Europe costs 12 Rs, a letter 20 Rs, both by airmail. Post offices are open *Mon–Fri 10am–6pm, Sat 10am–noon*.

TAXI

Almost all taxis are fitted with a meter, but try to negotiate a fixed price before-hand. On arrival at airports and stations, it's best to take a prepaid-taxi. Then there are no arguments about the price, or extras for luggage. A more economical alternative for short distances is the motorised-rickshaw, the *three-wheeler* or *tuk-tuk*. The same applies here: despite the occasional presence of a taximeter it's better to settle on a price first.

WEATHER IN GOA

	Jan	Feb	March	April	May	June	July	Aug	Sept	Oct	Nov	Dec
Daytime temperatures in °C/°F	32/90	32/90	30/86	33/91	33/91	30/86	29/84	29/84	29/84	31/88	33/91	33/91
Nighttime temperatures in °C/°F	20	20	23	25	26	24	24	24	24	24	22	20
☀ Sunshine hours/day	10	9	10	10	9	4	2	4	6	7	9	10
☂ Precipitation days/month	0	0	0	1	6	25	29	25	17	8	3	0
≋ Water temperature in °C/°F	27/81	27/81	28/82	29/84	29/84	28/82	27/81	27/81	27/81	28/82	28/82	27/81

TIME DIFFERENCE

India operates to one time zone. In winter it is 5.5 hours ahead of GMT (Greenwich Mean Time), in summer 4.5 hours ahead.

TIPPING

It is customary to tip waiters, porters, guides and drivers. The better the hotel, the more is expected. Tips are not included in bills. Always carry enough small change with you – people always want to be tipped.

TRAVEL AGENTS

IN THE UK

Audley Travel | *tel. 01993 838 000* | *www. audleytravel.com* (includes Classic Kerala in its India itineraries); Avion Holidays | *tel. 0208 449 7660* | *www.avionholidays. co.uk* (passionate about South India); Cox & Kings | *tel. 020 3813 9336* | *www.cox andkings.co.uk* (long-established exper-tise); Exodus | *tel. 0203 811 4260* | *www. exodus.co.uk* (adventure holiday specialists, including to South India); Kerala Connections | *tel. 01892 722440* | *www.ker alaconnections.co.uk* (tailor-made holidays in in Kerala, Tamil Nadu, Karnataka and Goa); Colours of India | *tel. 020 8347 4020* | *www.fb.com/Colours-of-India-73113293866* (India and South India specialists); Shoe-string | *tel. 01306 744797* | *www.shoestring. com* (for those on a tight budget); Trans Indus | *tel. 0844 879 3960* | *www.transindus. co.uk*; Voyage Jules Verne | *tel. 020 3811 6201* | *www.vjv.com*

IN INDIA

Also for tours, flights and accommodation throughout South India: *India Invites* | *Margao, Goa* | *tel. 0091 832 2 715781* | *www.indiainvites.com*; *Aries Travel & Holidays* | *Thiruvananthapuram, Kerala* | *tel. 0091 471 2 33 04 17* | *www.ariestravel.net* DER travel agency offers a round-trip through Rajasthan followed by a bathing holiday in Goa, only for women.

HINDI

Many of the following words are typical colloquial expressions used by Hindus and can seem unsuitable to Muslims.

Yes./no.	Dschi haa./Dschi nahi.	जी हाँ / जी नहीं
Yes. (Good, I understood)	Atschaa.	अच्छा.
Please./Thank you.	Krpaja./Than·kyuu.	कृपया. / धन्यवाद.
Sorry.	Maaf kii·ji·ye.	मुझे खेद है!
Good day!/Good evening!	Namastee!	नमस्ते!
Goodbye!	Namastee!	नमस्ते!
My name is ...	Mera namm ... hay.	मेरा नाम ... है.
How much does it cost?	Ye kitne paisse hay?	ये कितने पैसे हैं?
Excuse me, where is ...?	Dschi, kaha ... hay?	जी, कहाँ ... है?

1	ek	१ (एक)	5	pantsch	५ (पाँच)	9	no	८ (नौ)
2	do	२ (दो)	6	tschay	६ (छह)	10	das	१० (दस)
3	tin	३ (तीन)	7	ssaath	७ (सात)	20	bis	२० (बीस)
4	tschar	४ (चार)	8	aath	८ (आठ)	100	ssoh	१०० (सौ)

ROAD ATLAS

The green line indicates the Discovery Tour "India South at a glance"
The blue line indicates the other Discovery Tours

All tours are also marked on the pull-out map

Photo: Sri Meenakshi Temple in Madurai

Exploring India's South

The map on the back cover shows how the area has been sub-divided

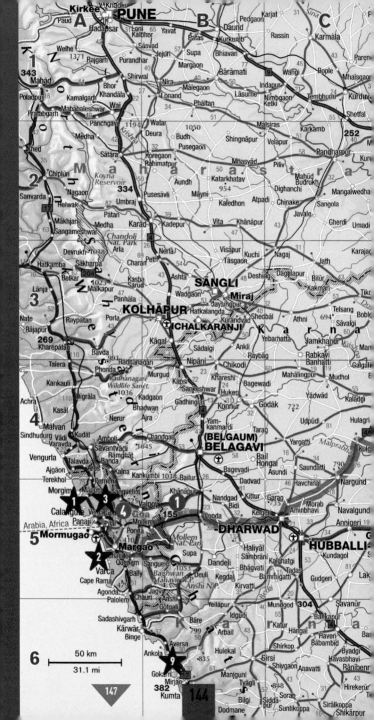

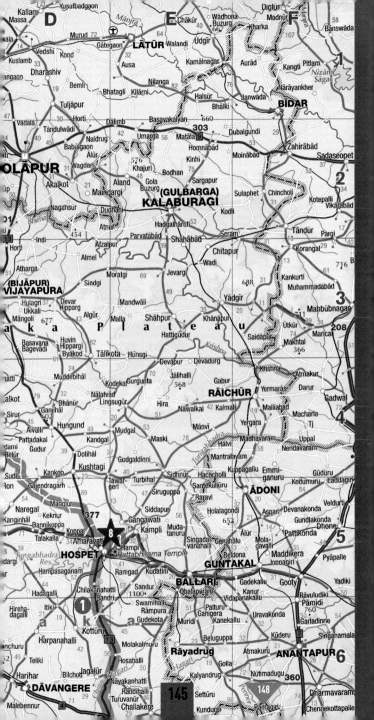

NOTES

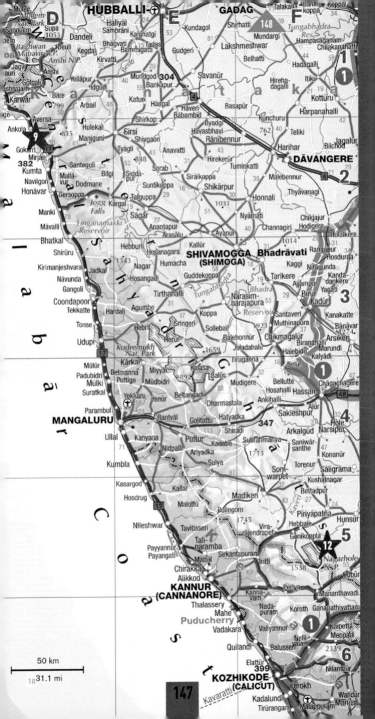

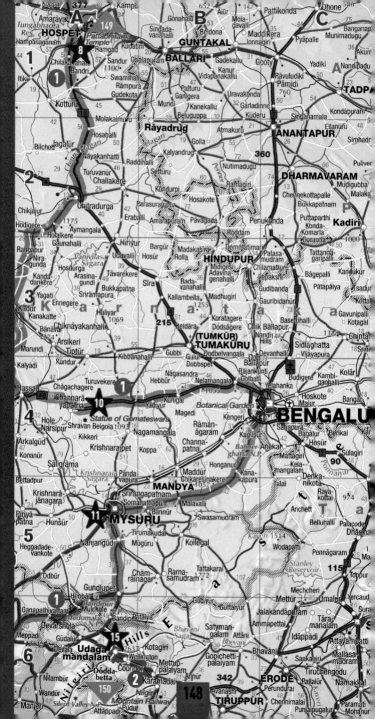

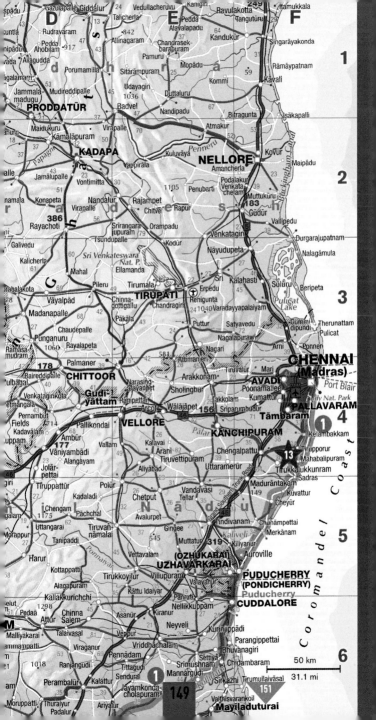

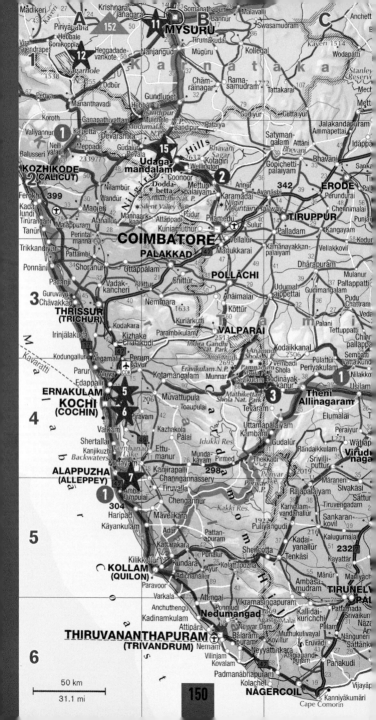

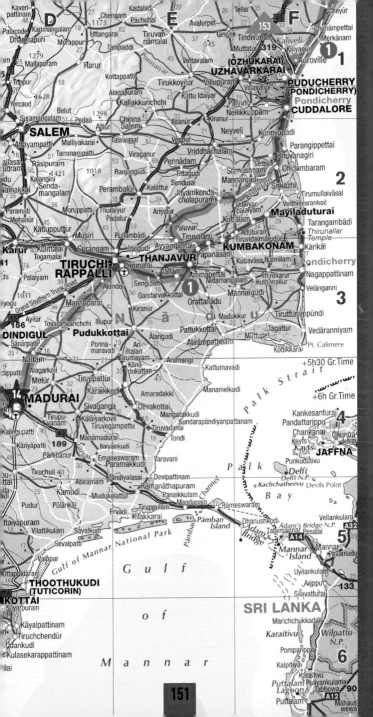

German	Symbol	French / Dutch
Autobahn, mehrspurige Straße - in Bau Highway, multilane divided road - under construction		Autoroute, route à plusieurs voies - en construction Autosnelweg, weg met meer rijstroken - in aanleg
Fernverkehrsstraße - in Bau Trunk road - under construction		Route à grande circulation - en construction Weg voor interlokaal verkeer - in aanleg
Hauptstraße Principal highway		Route principale Hoofdweg
Nebenstraße Secondary road		Route secondaire Overige verharde wegen
Fahrweg, Piste Practicable road, track		Chemin carrossable, piste Weg, piste
Straßennummerierung Road numbering	E20 81 70 26 5 40 9	Numérotage des routes Wegnummering
Entfernungen in Kilometer Distances in kilometers	259 130 129	Distances en kilomètres Afstand in kilometers
Höhe in Meter - Pass Height in meters - Pass	1365	Altitude en mètres - Col Hoogte in meters - Pas
Eisenbahn - Eisenbahnfähre Railway - Railway ferry		Chemin de fer - Ferry-boat Spoorweg - Spoorpont
Autofähre - Schifffahrtslinie Car ferry - Shipping route		Bac autos - Ligne maritime Autoveer - Scheepvaartlijn
Wichtiger internationaler Flughafen - Flughafen Major international airport - Airport		Aéroport importante international - Aéroport Belangrijke internationale luchthaven - Luchthaven
Internationale Grenze - Provinzgrenze International boundary - Province boundary		Frontière internationale - Limite de Province Internationale grens - Provinciale grens
Unbestimmte Grenze Undefined boundary		Frontière d'Etat non définie Rijksgrens onbepaalt
Zeitzonengrenze Time zone boundary	-4h Greenwich Time -3h Greenwich Time	Limite de fuseau horaire Tijdzone-grens
Hauptstadt eines souveränen Staates National capital	**MANILA**	Capitale nationale Hoofdstad van een souvereine staat
Hauptstadt eines Bundesstaates Federal capital	**Kuching**	Capitale d'un état fédéral Hoofdstad van een deelstat
Sperrgebiet Restricted area		Zone interdite Verboden gebied
Nationalpark National park		Parc national Nationaal park
Antikes Baudenkmal Ancient monument	∴	Monument antiques Antiek monument
Sehenswertes Kulturdenkmal Interesting cultural monument	∗ Angkor Wat	Monument culturel interéssant Bezienswaardig cultuurmonument
Sehenswertes Naturdenkmal Interesting natural monument	∗ Ha Long Bay	Monument naturel interéssant Bezienswaardig natuurmonument
Brunnen Well	⌣	Puits Bron
MARCO POLO Erlebnistour 1 MARCO POLO Discovery Tour 1		MARCO POLO Tour d'aventure 1 MARCO POLO Avontuurlijke Routes 1
MARCO POLO Erlebnistouren MARCO POLO Discovery Tours		MARCO POLO Tours d'aventure MARCO POLO Avontuurlijke Routes
MARCO POLO Highlight	★	MARCO POLO Highlight

MARCO POLO TRAVEL GUIDES

INDEX

The index includes all the places, excursion destinations and beaches, as well as important terms and persons described in the guide. Page numbers in bold indicate the main entry.

CREDITS

WRITE TO US

e-mail: info@marcopologuides.co.uk
Did you have a great holiday?
Is there something on your mind?
Whatever it is, let us know!
Whether you want to praise, alert us
to errors or give us a personal tip –
MARCO POLO would be pleased to
hear from you.
We do everything we can to provide the
very latest information for your trip.

Nevertheless, despite all of our authors'
thorough research, errors can creep in.
MARCO POLO does not accept any
liability for this. Please contact us by
e-mail or post.
MARCO POLO Travel Publishing Ltd
Pinewood, Chineham Business Park
Crockford Lane, Chineham
Basingstoke, Hampshire RG24 8AL
United Kingdom

PICTURE CREDITS
Cover photograph: Backwaters (Getty Images/travelstock 44/Look)
Photos: AWL Images: P. Adams (4 below, 66/67, 100/101, 103, 104, 114/115, 134 top), W. Bibikow (14/15, 49),
D. Delimont (93), M. Falzone (12/13, 25, 92, 146/147), P. Adams (109); AWL Images/Imagebroker (4 top, 9, 20/21, 29, 82, 94/95,
123, 134 below), P. Adams (109); AWL Images/John Warburton-Lee: A. Tozer (120); D. Gehm (1 below, 112); Getty
Images/travelstock 44/Look (1); huber-images: Ripani (87, 128 below), Schmid (flap left, 32/33, 37, 38, 43); Ishu
Datwani: Farrokh Chothia (19 below); O. Krüger (30/31, 40, 61, 71, 72, 75, 77, 80, 107, 110, 128 top, 129, 130, 132,
132/133, 133); Laif: Huber (52, 55, 79, 92/93), G. Knoll (18 top), Lewis (7); S. Laxminarayan/Dr. Vishwanath (19
top); K. Maeritz (130/131, 131); mauritius images/age fotostock / David H. Wells: D. H. Wells (30); mauritius
images/age fotostock: M. Turzak (11); mauritius images/Alamy (3, 6, 6, 7, 28 left, 2627), P. Bigg (22, 135), S.
Forster (59), J. Jochen Tack (65), C. Klodien (46), P. Quayle (34), C. Rangaraj (63), G. Rooney (5), O. Rupeta (87),
G. Taylor (31), C. Wakaskar (18 below), F. Werli (2); mauritius images/Alamy/ Dinodia Photos (18 centre); mauritius images/Alamy/ColsTravel (8); mauritius images/Alamy/Dinodia Photos (56); mauritius images/Axiom
Photographic: C. Caldicott (51), D. Kruell (44/45); mauritius images/Danita Delimont: W. Bibikow (99); mauri-
tius images/Foodanddrinkphotos (28 right); mauritius images/Hemis.fr: F. Guiziou (96); mauritius images/ib:
Krüger (91), Tack (85); mauritius images/Imagebroker: F. Bienewald (17), T. Seiter (89), V. Wolf (flap right); mauritius images/robertharding: L. Tettoni (10, 64); Schapowalow/4Corners: K. Richard (126/127); S. Verma (129)

2nd edition 2018 – fully revised and updated
Worldwide Distribution: Marco Polo Travel Publishing Ltd., Pinewood; Chineham Business Park, Crockford Lane,
Basingstoke, Hampshire RG24 8AL, UK. Email: sales@marcopolouk.com
© MAIRDUMONT GmbH & Co.KG, Ostfildern
Chief editor: Marion Zorn
Author: Dagmar Gehm; editor: Christina Sothmann; programme supervision: Lucas Forst-Gill, Susanne
Heimburger, Johanna Jiranek, Nikolai Michaelis, Martin Silbermann, Kristin Wittemann, Tim Wohlbold; picture
editor: Gabriele Forst; What's hot: Dagmar Gehm, wunder media, München
Cartography street atlas: © MAIRDUMONT, Ostfildern; carthography pull-out map: © MAIRDUMONT, Ostfildern
Cover design, p. 1, design pull-out map: Karl Anders – Büro für Visual Stories, Hamburg; Gestaltung innen:
milchhof:atelier, Berlin; Gestaltung Discovery Tours, p. 2/3: Susan Chaaban Dipl.-Des. (FH)
Translated from German by Tony Halliday, Oxford, and Suzanne Kirkbright, St Mary Bourne
Editorial office: SAW Communications, Redaktionsbüro Dr. Sabine A. Werner, Mainz: Julia Gilcher, Sariya Sloan,
Cosima Talhouni, Dr. Sabine A. Werner
Prepress: SAW Communications, Mainz, in cooperation with alles mit Medien, Mainz
Hindi box in cooperation with Ernst Klett Sprachen GmbH, Stuttgart,
Editorial by Pons Wörterbücher

MIX
Paper from
responsible sources
FSC® C124385

DOS & DON'TS ✋

A few things to bear in mind when travelling in South India

DON'T UNDERESTIMATE THE UNDERTOW

Regardless of whether you do water-sports or simply want to go swimming in the sea, it is vital to check out beforehand whether and where there is any dangerous undertow. When swimming, it's best to stick to the sections of beach designated as bathing areas and avoid unfamiliar waters.

DON'T BEHAVE AGGRESSIVELY

In India people react with complete bewilderment when foreigners raise their voices out of impatience or anger and lose their temper with others. Such behaviour is considered a sign of lack of self-control and as being uncouth. Go ahead and say clearly what the problem is, but without getting too agitated.

DON'T SHOW YOUR FEET

As many westerners can't sit cross-legged very well, after a while they tend to stretch out one or the other leg and almost inevitably end up pointing the sole of their foot towards somebody else. However, that is considered extremely impolite in India.

DON'T DRESS INAPPROPRIATELY

Nude sunbathing is officially forbidden, but many women tourists still take their tops off at the beach or pool. They shouldn't be surprised about any curious onlookers. Women who try to visit a temple with strap tops or short shorts will either be refused admission or lent some material with which to cover their shoulders and/or legs. Also adult women wearing mini-skirts evoke considerable disapproval. The same goes for men who enter hotels and restaurants without a shirt on. A good tip for women: with the salwar kameez – the long, loose-fitting tunic over tapering trousers – you'll always be dressed appropriately.

DON'T USE YOUR LEFT HAND

It is considered unclean. So only use the fingers of your right hand when you want to eat like the Indians do, namely without cutlery. The left hand stays firmly on your lap. Nor should gifts be presented with the left hand.

DON'T ENTER HOLY PLACES WEARING SHOES

It isn't just temples, pagodas and mosques that you shouldn't enter with shoes on, but museums and private houses as well. Getting your shoes looked after on dedicated shelves or counters only costs a few rupees. If you don't want to go barefoot, you can still wear socks.

DON'T DISPLAY AFFECTION IN PUBLIC

Indians are on the prudish side. Young couples now hold hands in public, but kissing and smooching outdoors are completely taboo. It violates the code of modesty, and holidaymakers should respect that.

Map Included